René Descartes

The World
&
Man

René Descartes

The World & Man

Edited and Translated by
Roger Ariew

Hackett Publishing Company, Inc.
Indianapolis/Cambridge

Copyright © 2023 by Hackett Publishing Company, Inc.

All rights reserved
Printed in the United States of America

26 25 24 23   1 2 3 4 5 6 7

For further information, please address
　　Hackett Publishing Company, Inc.
　　P.O. Box 44937
　　Indianapolis, Indiana 46244-0937

　　www.hackettpublishing.com

Cover design by Listenberger Design & Associates
Interior design by Laura Clark
Composition by Aptara, Inc.

Library of Congress Control Number: 2023932560

ISBN-13: 978-1-64792-133-0 (pbk.)
ISBN-13: 978-1-64792-137-8 (PDF ebook)

The paper used in this publication meets the minimum requirements of American National Standard for Information Sciences—Permanence of Paper for Printed Library Materials, ANSI Z39.48–1984.

∞

Contents

Introduction   *vii*

Part I. The World or Treatise on Light   1

  1. The Difference between Our Sensations and the Things That Produce Them   1

  2. What the Heat and Light of Fire Consists of   3

  3. Hardness and Liquidity   5

  4. The Void, and How It Happens That Our Senses Do Not Perceive Certain Bodies   8

  5. The Number of Elements and Their Qualities   11

  6. Description of a New World and the Qualities of the Matter of Which It Is Composed   15

  7. The Laws of Nature of This New World   18

  8. The Formation of the Sun and Stars of This New World   24

  9. The Origin and Course of the Planets and Comets in General, and Comets in Particular   28

  10. Planets in General, and the Earth and Moon in Particular   32

  11. Weight   36

  12. The Ebb and Flow of the Sea   40

  13. Light   42

  14. The Properties of Light   49

  15. That the Face of the Heaven of This New World Must Appear to Its Inhabitants Entirely Like That of Our World   53

Part II. Man   **61**

   1. The Machine of the Body   61

   2. How the Machine of the Body Moves   67

   3. The External Senses of This Machine and How They Are Related to Our External Senses   75

   4. On the Internal Senses of This Machine   89

   5. The Structure of the Brain of This Machine, and How the Spirits Are Distributed There to Cause Its Motions and Sensations   92

Appendix   **115**

   A. Descartes on Galileo, 1632–1638, Selected   115

   B. Descartes, *Discourse on Method*, Part V   124

   C. Summary of Descartes, *Description of the Human Body*   136

Introduction

René Descartes was born on March 31, 1596, at La Haye (now known as Descartes), in Touraine. He studied humanities, rhetoric, and philosophy at the Jesuit college at La Flèche, in Anjou (c. 1606–1614), then law at the University of Poitiers, receiving an M.A. in canon and civil law on November 9, 1616. Descartes subsequently enlisted as a gentleman soldier in the army of Maurice of Nassau, Prince of Orange, a Protestant ally of France during the war between the Netherlands and Spain, and spent 1618–1622 traveling through the Netherlands, Denmark, and Germany. He returned to France in 1622, abandoning his military career definitively, arriving in Paris in 1623. There he became acquainted or reacquainted with Marin Mersenne, an older student from La Flèche; Mersenne, who joined the Minims and resided at their convent in Paris, became Descartes's primary correspondent on all matters philosophical, scientific, and mathematical. Descartes lived mostly in Paris until he left for the Netherlands, where he remained for some twenty years, except for three trips to France (1644, 1647, and 1648); in the end, he went to the court of Queen Christina of Sweden in September 1649 and died not long after, on February 11, 1650.

The exact date of Descartes's arrival in the Netherlands is not known. It was preceded by a brief visit in October 1628, after which he returned in February or March 1629. He may not have meant to remain there permanently; initially, he intended merely to finish some projects he started in Paris (such as working on a machine for grinding hyperbolic lenses), for which he needed quiet and privacy, something he could not find in France.[1] Many have speculated about why the French Catholic Descartes

---

[1]. Descartes said in a letter: "However perfect a country house may be, it always lacks an infinity of comforts that can be found only in towns; and even the solitude one hopes to find in it never turns out to be completely perfect. [. . .] It can happen that you also have a quantity of petty neighbors who will bother you at times, and their visits will be even more annoying than the ones you receive in Paris. Instead, in this large town in which I live [Amsterdam], everybody trades in merchandise, except for me, and thus each is so attentive to his own profit that I could live all my life here without ever being noticed by anyone. I take a walk every day amid the bustle of a large crowd, with as much freedom and tranquility as you would in your garden paths, and I pay no more attention to the people I see there

would want to live in a Protestant country such as the Netherlands. It should be sufficient to note the peace and freedom he would derive there, far from the court, his friends, and relatives. With the birth of his daughter Francine, with Helena Jans, on July 19, 1635, he would have had additional reasons to remain.[2]

It is clear, moreover, that Descartes's stay in the Netherlands was most productive intellectually. In a letter to Mersenne written just over a year after his arrival, he claimed to have discovered the foundations of physics by using his reason to try to know God and the self. As he said, "The first nine months I was in this country I worked at nothing else." He even asserted that he thought he "found out how one can demonstrate the truths of metaphysics in a way that is more evident than the demonstrations of Geometry."[3] But, he said, he did not consider it appropriate to publish this work, his *Little Treatise on Metaphysics*, "in which the main points are to prove *the existence of God* and that of *our souls*, when they are separate from the body, from which their immortality follows,"[4] until he first saw how his physics would be received. Thus, by April 15, 1630, Descartes had announced to Mersenne that he had resolved to his satisfaction the foundations of his physics based on a forerunner of his metaphysics, something he later published in various forms as *Discourse on Method*, Part IV (1637), *Meditations on First Philosophy* (1641), and *Principles of Philosophy*, Part I (1644).

Thinking about the foundations of physics based on metaphysical considerations were new endeavors for Descartes since, in the same April 15, 1630, letter, he declared to Mersenne that he had put away the projects he had been working on when he was in France:

---

than I would to the trees in your forests or to the animals grazing there," Descartes to Guez de Balzac [May 1631], in *Oeuvres de Descartes*, 2nd ed, ed. Charles Adam and Paul Tannery (Paris: Vrin, 1996), vol. I, 203. Henceforth, this edition is abbreviated AT. Page number references to the AT edition are given in the margins. Throughout this book, dates enclosed in parentheses appear in the letters; dates enclosed in brackets are conjectured.

2. Francine died of scarlet fever on September 7, 1640. In 1644, Helena Jans married a local innkeeper with a sizeable dowry provided by Descartes.

3. Descartes to Mersenne (April 15, 1630), AT I, 144.

4. Descartes to Mersenne [November 25, 1630], AT I, 182. Descartes's *Little Treatise on Metaphysics* is lost.

> Perhaps you find it strange that I started some other treatises when I was in Paris which I did not continue. I will tell you the reason for this: when I was working on them I gained a little more knowledge than I had when I started them, and wanting to take this into account, I was forced to start a new project, one a little larger than the first; in the same way, if someone who started building a house for himself acquired some unexpected wealth and changed his status, such that the building he started was now too small for him, we would not blame him if we saw him start another house more suitable to his fortune.[5]

He also referred to a small treatise on physics he had started, which, he said, he was working on very slowly "because I take a lot more pleasure in learning by myself than in writing down what little I know. I am now studying chemistry and anatomy at the same time, and every day I learn something I cannot find in books." He also told Mersenne that he resolved "to put it in such a state that I may send it to you by the beginning of year 1633."[6]

The Beginnings of The World

Six months earlier, in summer 1629, Descartes had become intrigued with the reported phenomenon of parhelia, or false suns, observed by the Jesuit Christopher Scheiner on March 20, 1629, and began working on optics and physics. In a letter of October 8, 1629, he said to Mersenne:

> Just over two months ago one of my friends showed me here a fairly full description of the phenomenon and asked me what I thought about it. I had to interrupt what I had in hand to examine all meteors[7] in

---

5. Descartes to Mersenne (April 15, 1630), AT I, 137–38. It is not clear which treatises Descartes started in Paris that he is not continuing; apart from some fragments of mathematics and mathematical physics, there are two large unfinished treatises by Descartes dating from that time among the papers recovered after he died: the *Studium Bonae Mentis* (*Study of the Good Mind*, now lost) and *Regulae ad Directionem Ingenii* (*Rules for the Direction of the Ingenium*, published posthumously in Latin, 1701). The beginning of the *Dioptrics* clearly also dates from this period.

6. Descartes to Mersenne (April 15, 1630), AT I, 137.

7. "Meteors" traditionally refers to phenomena or objects below the moon, that is, in the air, water, or earth. Descartes's *Meteors*, published with the *Discourse on Method*, treats: 1. The Nature of Terrestrial Bodies; 2. Vapors and Exhalations; 3. Salt; 4. Winds; 5. Clouds; 6.

succession before I could be satisfied with an answer. But I now think I can account for it somewhat and I decided to compose a small treatise about the topic, which will contain the reason for the colors of the rainbow—a topic that has given me more trouble than any other—and generally the reason for all sublunary phenomena.[8]

In the same letter, Descartes asked Mersenne to send him other descriptions of the phenomenon to see whether they agreed with the one he had. He told Mersenne that he decided to publish the results of his inquiry anonymously as a specimen of his philosophy and requested his help in publishing the treatise in Paris: "I would send it to you when it is finished, as much to correct it as to put it in the hands of a publisher." In an aside, he replied to Mersenne that he agreed with the account of rarefaction Mersenne told him about: "As for rarefaction, I agree with this physician, and I have now taken a position regarding all the foundations of philosophy; but perhaps I do not explain the ether as he does."[9] Thus Descartes's claims about having settled on the foundations of philosophy or physics, that is, the beginnings of *The World*, date from the summer of 1629, not long after he first arrived in the Netherlands. A month later, Descartes was busy working on the treatise and had already expanded its scope to "all of Physics." He thanked Mersenne for sending him the second description of parhelia and agreeing to see to the printing of the treatise he was writing. He added,

but I should tell you it will not be ready for more than a year. For, since I wrote to you a month ago, I did nothing more than sketch the argument and, instead of explaining just one phenomenon, I decided to explain all the phenomena of nature, that is, the whole of physics. This plan pleases me more than any other I ever had, for I think I see how to expound all my thoughts in a way that some will find satisfying and others will not have the occasion to contradict.[10]

Snow, Rain, and Hail; 7, Storms, Lightning, and All Other Fires Blazing in the Air; 8. The Rainbow; 9. The Color of Clouds and Circles or Coronas That We Sometime See around the Heavenly Bodies; and 10. The Apparition of Several Suns.

8. Descartes to Mersenne (October 8, 1629), AT I, 23–24.

9. Descartes to Mersenne (October 8, 1629), AT I, 23–24. The physician is likely to be Sebastian Basso in his *Philosophia naturalis adversus Aristotelem* (Geneva, 1621).

10. Descartes to Mersenne (November 13, 1629), AT I, 70.

A subsequent letter to Mersenne elaborated on Descartes's concerns about the subjects he was treating. He told Mersenne that before sending the treatise to the printers, he would like it to be thoroughly examined by Mersenne and any other able people who would be willing to take the trouble to do so. As Descartes explained:

> I want this mainly because of theology, which has been so subjugated to Aristotle that it is almost impossible to explain another philosophy without it seeming at the outset against the faith. And regarding this, please let me know if there is anything which has been determined by religion concerning the extent of created things, that is, whether it is finite or rather infinite, and whether there are real created bodies in all these regions called imaginary spaces. For, although I did not want to touch upon this issue, I believe however that I will be forced to prove something regarding it.[11]

Descartes's concerns about religious issues persisted. Discussing the relations between his treatise on physics, now called *The World*, and his treatise on optics, that is, the *Dioptrics*, he indicated an overlap in the two works regarding the theory of colors. And he insisted that he would finish his *World* within three years:

> I want to insert in it a discourse in which I will try to explain the nature of colors and light. This held me up for six months and it is not yet half finished; but it will be longer than I thought and contain almost a complete physics. Thus, I am hoping it will serve to discharge me from the promise I made you, to finish my *World* in three years, given that it will almost be a summary of it. The fable of my *World* pleases me too much to fail to complete it. [. . .] I think I will send you this discourse on light as soon as it is complete, before sending you the rest of the *Dioptrics*.[12]

He alluded in the letter to a theological issue he would need to resolve in his treatise about how his explanation of colors might affect the naturalistic explanation of the sacrament of the Eucharist: "Wanting to describe colors in my fashion in it [that is, in the *Dioptrics* and hence also in

---

11. Descartes to Mersenne (December 18, 1629), AT I, 86–87.
12. Descartes to Mersenne [November 25, 1630], AT I, 179. Descartes adds a few lines later: "I am not in a hurry to finish the *Dioptrics*."

The World] and consequently being obliged to explain how the whiteness of the bread remains in the Blessed Sacrament, I would be glad to have it examined by my friends before it is seen by the whole world."[13]

A few months later, Descartes told Mersenne that he was making some slow progress and that he was describing the beginning of his imagined world, which would contain much of his physics. He related that he was rereading the first chapter of Genesis and "discovered as if by miracle, that it can be much better explained following my imaginations, it seems to me, than in all the ways the exegetes explain it, something I had no hope for until now. But now I propose to myself, after having explained my new philosophy, to show clearly that it agrees with all truths of the Faith much better than Aristotle's philosophy."[14] Still, Descartes's task seemed enormous. He needed to resolve numerous issues in various domains, such as philosophy, physics, and religion. As he said:

> I am now set on untangling the chaos to bring out light from it, which is one of the loftiest and the most difficult matters I could ever undertake, as almost all of physics is comprised in it. I have a thousand different things to consider all together to find a means by which I can speak the truth without shocking the imagination of anyone nor offending the opinions received by all.[15]

Descartes also recognized that he needed more observational data to resolve his mass of problems. He asked Mersenne whether there were books with new data on the motion of the sunspots and that of the moons of Jupiter and Saturn.[16] Mersenne sent him some unpublished observations by Pierre Gassendi, but he wanted to know more:

> I would like to know in general whether he was able to see many sunspots and how many he saw at the same time; whether they all went at the same speed and whether their shape always appears to be round. I would also like to know whether he observed for certain that the refraction of the air made the stars appear elevated more highly when near the

---

13. Descartes to Mersenne [November 25, 1630], AT I, 179.
14. Descartes to [Mersenne] [early 1631], AT IV, 697.
15. Descartes to Mersenne (December 23, 1630), AT I, 194.
16. Descartes to Mersenne (December 18, 1629), AT I, 102–3.

horizon than they are in fact. Assuming he observed this, whether this refraction also occurs with the moon; also, if the refraction is greater or smaller with stars close to the northern horizon than with those toward the south. These things require instruments so accurate and calculations so exact that I cannot dare hope anybody has been able to determine them definitely; but if there is someone who can do it, I know of no one in whom I have greater hope than him.[17]

By the spring of 1632, Descartes was still working on *The World* and looking for observational data. He wrote to Mersenne that the treatise was almost finished but that he wanted to keep it for a few more months because he needed to "revise it and make a clean copy, and to draw some figures necessary for it"; he also referred to some experiments he conducted himself—"supplementing reasoning with experience"—saying: "This is what distracted me these last days; for I occupied myself in making various experiments to discover the essential differences between oils, spirits or alcohols, ordinary waters, acidic waters, salts, etc."[18] In another letter, he requested information about comets:

If you know of some author who specifically collected various observations made of comets, you will oblige me also to inform me of it. For, I was very committed to studying the heavens in the last two or three months; and after I satisfied myself concerning its nature and that of the stars we see in it, and many other things I did not dare to hope only a few years ago, I became so bold that I now dare seek the cause of the position of every fixed star. For although they seem quite irregularly scattered here and there in the heavens, I have no doubt, however, that there is a regular and determinate natural order among them. [. . .] Now I find nothing that might better help me to achieve the knowledge of that order than the observations of many comets. [. . .] So, I would be pleased to find someone who collected all together what I cannot without great trouble draw from individual authors, each of whom wrote about only a comet or two.[19]

---

17. Descartes to Mersenne (January 1630), AT I, 112–13.
18. Descartes to Mersenne [April 5, 1632], AT I, 243.
19. Descartes to Mersenne [May 10, 1632], AT I, 250–51.

Descartes understood that he would not find the kinds of accounts he was looking for. Still, he mused about whether there might be somebody who might be pleased to work for the advancement of science and conduct experiments at their own expense. He dreamt of a person, working in the fashion of Francis Bacon, who would be willing "without putting forth any reasons or hypotheses, to describe the sky to us exactly, as it appears now, and the situation of every fixed star with respect to its neighbours, what difference, whether in size, colour or clarity, or in being more or less sparkling, etc."[20] He continued, asking for his imagined observer to annotate the observations: the observer should indicate if his observations met with what the ancient astronomers wrote about them and what differences were found; he should add to them observations of comets, putting the path of each one in a small table, as Tycho Brahe did for the comets he observed;[21] and finally, he should append the variations in the planets' ecliptic paths and apogees. Descartes concluded that such a work "would be more useful to the public than it would perhaps seem at first and would relieve me of much bother."[22]

In June 1632, Descartes announced another extension of *The World* and, at the same time, revealed the abandonment of an even larger extension of it:

> It has been a month since I have been deliberating about whether I would describe in my *World* how animals are generated, and I finally resolved myself to do nothing about it anymore, as it would take me too long. I finished all I planned to include in it concerning inanimate bodies. The only thing I have left is to add something concerning the nature of man, and afterward I will produce a clean copy to send to you.

---

20. Descartes to Mersenne [May 10, 1632], AT I, 251–52.

21. Referring to Tycho Brahe in his *De Mundi Aetherei Recentioribus Phaenomenis Liber Secundus* (Prague, 1603).

22. Descartes to Mersenne [May 10, 1632], AT I, 251–52. The more realistic Descartes actually concludes: "But I do not expect it will be done, nor do I expect to find what I am looking for now concerning the stars. I believe it is a science that surpasses the scope of the human mind; however, I am so unwise I cannot prevent myself from dreaming about it, even though I judge it will only result in my wasting some time, as I already did for the past two months, such that I did not progress at all on my Treatise. But I will still have it done before the deadline I related to you."

But I do not dare say when that will be, for I already broke my promises so many times I am ashamed of it.[23]

A year later, he was still working on his expanded project, writing to Mersenne that he read William Harvey's book on the motion of the heart and circulation of the blood, which Mersenne once suggested to him:[24]

> I will speak in my *World* about man a bit more than I thought I would, because I am undertaking to explain all of man's principal functions. I already wrote about those belonging to life, such as digestion of food, the beating of the pulse, the distribution of nourishment, etc., and the five senses. I am now dissecting the heads of various animals to explain in what the imagination, memory, etc., consist in. I saw the book, *On the Motion of the Heart*, which you once mentioned to me, and I found myself differing a little from his opinion.[25]

The same letter from the end of 1632 contained a short discussion of Galileo's *Two Chief World Systems*, whose contents Mersenne was relating to Descartes. Descartes rejected Galileo's calculation of the speed of falling bodies[26] as not bearing any relation to his philosophy, and asked about Galileo's explanation of the tides: "I would like to know what he writes of the ebb and flow of the sea, because it is one of the things that gave me the most difficulties to discover. Although I think I achieved this, there are however circumstances of which I am not aware."[27] In July 1633, Descartes again announced that his treatise was almost completed but that he still needed to correct and copy it. This time, however, he claimed that he did not have to look for anything new and that he still wanted to keep his promise to deliver the treatise to Mersenne before the end of the year.[28]

---

23. Descartes to Mersenne [June 1632], AT I, 254.
24. William Harvey, *Exercitatio anatomica de Motu Cordis et Sanguinis in animalibus* (Frankfurt, 1628).
25. Descartes to Mersenne [November–December 1632], AT I, 263.
26. Galileo's *Massimi sistemi del mondo* (*Dialogue Concerning the Two Chief World Systems*, Florence, 1632) is divided into four Days; the speed of falling bodies is calculated by Galileo in the Second Day.
27. Descartes to Mersenne [November–December 1632], AT I, 261 (see Appendix A.1). Galileo's theory of the tides is developed in the Fourth Day of *Two Chief World Systems*.
28. Descartes to Mersenne (July 22, 1633), AT I, 268.

The End of The World

In late November 1633, as he was preparing *The World* for publication, Descartes heard that Galileo had been condemned by the Catholic Church the previous June for defending the motion of the earth. Descartes had gone to booksellers in Leiden and Amsterdam to look for a copy of Galileo's book, published in Florence in 1632, and was told that it had indeed been printed, but all copies were burned in Rome, and Galileo had a fine imposed on him. His reaction to the news was swift and powerful:

> This so shocked me I almost resolved myself to burn all of my papers, or at least not to let anyone see them. For I could not imagine that he, an Italian, and even well-liked by the Pope, as far as I understand, could be made a criminal for anything other than his wanting, no doubt, to establish the motion of the earth, which I know was already censored by some Cardinals.[29]

Descartes canceled the publication of his own treatise containing the proposition deemed heretical because, he said, "if this view is false, all the foundations of my philosophy are as well, because it is evidently demonstrated by them. And it is so linked with all the parts of my Treatise that I would not know how to detach it without rendering the rest completely defective." He added: "I would never, for anything in the world, want a discourse to come from me in which even the least word disapproved of by the Church could be found."[30]

Although we have a copy of his letter to Mersenne detailing these thoughts about the matter, that letter seems not to have arrived in Paris. A few months later, not having heard from Mersenne, Descartes started another letter to him, repeating what he had said about his decision to suppress *The World*: "The knowledge I have of your virtue gives me hope you will not have anything but the best opinion of me, given that I wanted to suppress entirely the Treatise I wrote and lose almost all of my four years of work by giving complete obedience to the Church in its prohibition of the opinion of the earth's motion." And he probed about the status of Galileo's condemnation in France: "All the same, because I did not yet see that either the Pope or the Council ratified this prohibition (it was

---

29. Descartes to Mersenne [late November 1633], AT I, 270–71 (see Appendix A.2).
30. Descartes to Mersenne [late November 1633], AT I, 271 (see Appendix A.2).

made only by the Congregation of Cardinals established for the censure of books), I would be very happy to learn what is now held of this in France, and if their authority was sufficient to make it an article of faith."[31] Presumably, Descartes received a new letter from Mersenne before he sent him this last letter, and so he replaced it with one that directly addressed Mersenne's new letter, repeating what he had said in the lost letter.[32]

Descartes's decision to stop the publication of *The World*, as written at the time, seemed firm, although he continued to probe the reasons for Galileo's condemnation. He understood that defending the motion of the earth was something already censored by high members of the church; that was done in 1616.[33] But Descartes, and presumably Galileo, should have been able to abide by such a prohibition by not explicitly defending the censured proposition. Descartes, at least, was writing a "fable," an account of a world that God, if he wished, could create in some of the imaginary spaces beyond this world. This was something Descartes believed from the start he could safely expound, and such that, as we already pointed out, "some will find satisfying and others will not have the occasion to contradict."[34] However, Descartes had not yet read Galileo's book and did not know how he approached the matter; as he said to Mersenne, as late as May 15, 1634: "And since you saw Galileo's book, I also ask you to tell me what it contains and what you judged were the motives for his condemnation." He further asked Mersenne about his reporting that a churchman wrote a treatise establishing the motion of the earth: "I also ask you to tell me the name of the treatise you said was recently written by a churchman proving the motion of the earth—at least whether it was published."[35] Descartes was astonished that a man of the church would dare to write about the motion of the earth, however he excused himself, because the reason for Galileo's condemnation had become manifest to

---

31. Descartes to Mersenne [February 1634] AT I, 281 (see Appendix A.3).
32. Descartes to Mersenne [late February 1634], AT I, 285 (see Appendix A.4).
33. See the documents provided in Galileo Galilei, *The Essential Galileo*, ed. and trans. M. Finocchiaro (Indianapolis: Hackett Publishing, 2008), 168–78.
34. Descartes to Mersenne (November 13, 1629), AT I, 70.
35. Descartes to Mersenne (May 15, 1634), AT I, 298 (see Appendix A.6). The churchman was Ismael Boulliau, whose defense of Copernicanism, *Philolai, sive Dissertationis de vero systemate mundi*, was not published until 1639.

Descartes even before he had read Galileo's book;[36] it was clear that the same reason would apply to him as to the churchman: "I saw letters patent for the condemnation of Galileo, printed at Liege on September 20, 1633, in which are the words *although he pretended he was putting it forward only hypothetically*. Thus, they seem even to be forbidding the use of that hypothesis in astronomy. This prevents me from daring to communicate to him any of my thoughts on this subject."[37] Descartes correctly judged that it was not the right time to discuss the prohibited proposition, even hypothetically, that is, even in a dialogue or as a fable. Still, such a prohibition could be lifted in the future, and there was at least one precedent for this. As Descartes said:

> Moreover, since I do not yet see that this censure was authorized by the Pope or by the Council, but only by a particular congregation of Cardinal Inquisitors, I do not wholly lose hope that the same thing will happen in this case that happened with the antipodes, which were formerly condemned in pretty much the same manner, and thus that, with time, my *World* will be able to see the light.[38]

On August 12, 1634, Descartes was finally able to read Galileo's book for himself: "Mr [Isaac] Beeckman came here Saturday night and loaned me Galileo's book, but he took it back to Dordrecht this morning, so I had it in my hands for only 30 hours. I was able to flip through the whole book."[39] His opinion of the book was mixed. He clearly did not approve of Galileo's explanation of the tides as a phenomenon that could be explained solely through the motion of the earth, without reference to the moon.

---

36. See Descartes to Mersenne [around May 1, 1634], AT I, 288 (see Appendix A.5).

37. Descartes to Mersenne [around May 1, 1634], AT I, 288 (see Appendix A.5). Descartes quotes the Liege text in a subsequent letter—see Descartes to Mersenne (August 14, 1634), AT I, 306 (see Appendix A.7). The text makes it clear that the Sacred Tribunal of the Inquisition concluded that Galileo merely pretended that he was proposing the condemned proposition only as a hypothesis. Galileo was strongly suspected of heresy insofar as he held a false doctrine or believed that it could be defended as probable.

38. Descartes to Mersenne [around May 1, 1634], AT I, 288 (see Appendix A.5). Descartes is referring to the Condemnation of Vergilius, abbot of St. Peter's and later bishop of Salzburg, by Pope Zachary in 748.

39. Descartes to Mersenne (August 14, 1634), AT I, 303–4 (see Appendix A.7). The book, of course, is Galileo's *Two Chief World Systems*, 1632. August 14, 1634, was a Monday, the usual day when the mail carrier took Descartes's letters addressed for Paris.

And he formulated a criticism he elaborates on in a later account of Galileo's subsequent book, *Two New Sciences*:

> I find he philosophizes well enough about motion, even though he has very little to say about it I find entirely true. But as for what I can see, he is more deficient when he follows received opinions than when he deviates from them, except, however, when he discusses the ebb and flow of the tides, which I find to be a bit far-fetched. I also explained this by the motion of the earth in my *World*, but in a way completely different than his. [. . .] His arguments to prove the motion of the earth are very good. But it seems to me that he does not present them as he should to make them persuasive, as the digressions he mixes in between are the reason the first arguments are not remembered when the last ones are read.[40]

Descartes's decision not to publish *The World* or anything else that might be controversial did not entail that he should stop all his work on his various scientific treatises. By the following spring, he related to Mersenne that he had worked on his earlier project, the *Dioptrics*, which had become interwoven with *The World*: "Since the condemnation of Galileo, I revised and completely finished the Treatise I started earlier. Having entirely separated it from my *World*, I intend to print it by itself in a short while."[41] Ultimately, he determined "that it was easy for me to choose some matters that, without being subject to much controversy nor obliging me to declare more of my principles than I desire, would nevertheless allow me to show quite clearly what I can or cannot do in the sciences."[42] Hence, in October 1635, Descartes decided to publish the *Dioptrics*, adding the *Meteors* to the project in November, and resolving to set off the two treatises with a short preface. The project took greater shape in March 1636 when Descartes reported that he would include some other works as well; as he said, he wished to publish anonymously "four Treatises all in French, and the general title will be: *The Project of a Universal Science That Can Elevate Our Nature to Its Highest Degree of Perfection. Then the Dioptrics, Meteors, and Geometry, in Which the Most*

---

40. Descartes to Mersenne (August 14, 1634), AT I, 304–5 (see Appendix A.7). For Descartes's general critique of Galileo's *Two New Sciences*, see Descartes to Mersenne [October 11, 1638], AT II, 380 (see Appendix A.12).

41. Descartes to [Mersenne] [March 1635], AT I, 322 (see Appendix A.8).

42. *Discourse on Method*, Part VI, AT VI, 75.

Curious Matters That the Author Could Have Chosen to Serve as Proof of the Universal Science He Proposes Are Explained in Such a Way That Even Those Who Have Never Studied Can Understand Them." At this time, he was representing the introductory materials as: "In this *Project* I reveal a part of my Method, I undertake to demonstrate the existence of God and of the soul separated from the body, and I add to it several other things I believe will not be unpleasant to the reader."[43] Clearly, the plan grew from there. Eventually, Descartes published the work as *Discourse on the Method for Conducting One's Reason Well and for Seeking the Truth in the Sciences*, in six parts, together with *Dioptrics*, *Meteors*, and *Geometry*. He also indicated that he "inserted some things of metaphysics, physics, and medicine to show that the method extends to all kinds of subjects."[44] *Discourse*, Part IV contained his metaphysics, what will become the *Meditations* and *Principle of Philosophy*, Part I; *Discourse*, Part V contained a summary of parts of *The World* and *Man*.[45]

This was the end of the project that started in 1629. Occasionally, the publication of *The World* came up again, but Descartes saw no change that might alter his decision; as he said to Mersenne on June 19, 1639: "I did not reply to Mr [Florimond] Debeaune concerning the publication of my *World*; for I had nothing to reply, except that, since the causes that prevented me from doing so did not change, I must not change my resolution."[46] And the reasons for his resolution also did not change; as he told Mersenne in December 1640: "if you write to Cardinal di Bagno's physician, I would be very glad if you inform him that nothing prevented me until now from publishing my philosophy than the prohibition of the motion of the earth, which I could not separate from my philosophy

---

43. Descartes to Mersenne [March 1636], AT I, 339.
44. Descartes to Mersenne [April 1637], AT I, 349.
45. See Appendix B.
46. Descartes to Mersenne (June 19, 1639), AT II, 565. Descartes added: "However, in this regard, please let me know whether the copies that Mr the Nuncio promised you to keep for Cardinal di Bagno, etc. were finally addressed; for I have reason to doubt that the difficulty they had to be carried there came from the fear that they might be treating the motion of the earth; it has been more than two years since Maire, having offered to send copies to a bookseller in Rome, he replied that he wanted a dozen of them, as long as there was nothing in them that concerned the motion of the earth; and since then, having received them, he sent them, or at least wanted to send them, to that country."

because all my physics depends on it."⁴⁷ Still, Descartes continued to probe about the status of the condemnation. Sometime later, writing to an unknown correspondent, he declared that "with respect to sacred theology and the true religion, I am sure there is nothing to which my philosophy does not square more easily than common philosophy." He added, however, "there remains only one scruple, about the motion of the earth. I took care to consult on this topic with a Cardinal who professes to be a friend of mine for many years and is one of the members of the congregation that condemned Galileo. I will know from him what is permitted and what is not."⁴⁸

The World *Reborn*

After the publication of the *Discourse on Method*, in which he had announced that he would be very pleased to have his writings examined and that the resulting criticism could be sent to his publisher to be printed,⁴⁹ Descartes received numerous objections to the *Discourse* and its appended treatises, the *Dioptrics*, *Meteors*, and *Geometry*. He was not particularly happy about either the quantity or the quality of the objections, but he was kept very busy answering them.⁵⁰ One lengthy set of objections by the

---

47. Descartes to Mersenne [December 1640], AT III, 258–59. Descartes added: "Please ask him to sound out the Cardinal on this subject, because being most deeply his servant, I would be very sorry to displease him, and having much zeal for the Catholic religion, I generally revere all its leaders. I will not add that I do not want to put myself at risk of their censure; for, believing very strongly in the infallibility of the Church and having no doubt about my reasons, I cannot fear that one truth may be contrary to the other."

48. Descartes to unknown [1641–1644], AT V, 544.

49. *Discourse on Method*, Part VI, AT VI, 75.

50. The extant mass of Descartes's correspondence from 1638 exceeded all previous correspondence. Given that some summaries of *The World* and *Man* were published in the *Discourse on Method*, they received comments from readers of the *Discourse on Method* to which Descartes replied. Topics such as animals as machines and the circulation of the blood were foremost among these. For questions about animal machines, see, for example, portions of S. P. to [Reneri] for Descartes [April 1638], with Descartes's answer, Descartes to [Reneri] for S. P. [May 1638], as well as Descartes to [Newcastle] [November 23, 1646]; and parts of the exchange with More: More to Descartes (December 11, 1648), Descartes to More (February 5, 1649), More to Descartes (March 5, 1649), and Descartes to More (April 15, 1649). For questions about the motion of the heart and circulation of the blood, see the exchanges with V. F. Plemp—including portions of Fromondus to Plemp (September 13, 1637) and Descartes to Plemp for Fromondus [October 3, 1637]—that is, Plemp to

mathematician and engineer Pierre Petit about *Discourse*, Part IV and the *Dioptrics* rankled him more than the others.[51] Descartes initially said that he did not take Petit seriously but simply mocked him in response.[52] Still, Petit's objections to *Discourse*, Part IV motivated Descartes to expound upon what he had published of his metaphysical thoughts (that is, to write the *Meditations*). A recently discovered letter to Mersenne indicates that, until very late, the *Meditations* were intended to be introduced by a Latin translation of *Discourse*, Part IV, and then a preface responding to Petit; Descartes removed these and inserted instead the current Preface to the Reader. As he said:

> I was forced to soften what I had written about Mr. Petit, as you will see in the preface to the reader, which I sent you to have printed, if you please, at the beginning of the book after the dedicatory Epistle to the faculty of the Sorbonne, and not to print the 4th part of the *Discourse on Method* or the small preface I put after it, nor the one that preceded the objections of the Theologian but only the Synopsis.[53]

Descartes (September 15, 1637), Descartes to Plemp (October 3, 1637), Descartes to Plemp (December 20, 1637), Plemp to Descartes [January 1638], Descartes to Plemp (February 15, 1638), Plemp to Descartes [March 1638], Descartes to Plemp (March 23, 1638), and Descartes to [Plemp] [August 1638?]. See also Van Beverwijck to Descartes (June 10, 1643) and Descartes to Van Beverwijck (July 5, 1643).

51. Petit to Descartes via Mersenne [March 12, 1638] and [May 1, 1638], not in AT. See Cornelis de Waard, "Les objections de Pierre Petit contre le *Discours* et les *Essais* de Descartes," *Revue de Métaphysique et de Morale* 32 (1925): 70–81.

52. Descartes said to Mersenne, "As for Mr Petit, I did not at all approve of his writing, and I judged that he wanted to join the party, and to present objections without however having anything to object to. He did nothing more but throw in several boring commonplaces, borrowed for the most part from the atheists, which he piles up without judgment, confining himself primarily to what I wrote about God and the soul—not one word of which he understood" (May 27, 1638), AT II, 135. Also: "As for Mr Petit, he only showed that he wanted to be contrary without understanding a thing about what he was attacking. However, given that he mainly limited himself to what I wrote about the existence of God, I resolved to write an essay full of derision in responding to him. But, because this subject is too serious to be mixed in with jokes, I will let him off more lightly," Descartes to Mersenne [June 29, 1638], AT II, 191–92. And: "I would have no less shame in writing against this kind of man than stopping and pursuing some small dog barking at me on a street," Descartes to Mersenne (July 27, 1638), AT II, 267.

53. *Descartes to Mersenne*, May 27, 1641; not in AT. See Erik-Jan Bos, "Two Unpublished Letters of René Descartes: On the Printing of the Meditations and the Groningen Affair,"

We can note as well the beginnings of the *Meditations* as early as July 1638, in the context of the dispute with Petit.[54] A few months later, the project had progressed considerably; Descartes said to Mersenne: "I now have in my hands a discourse in which I try to clarify what I previously wrote on this subject [the existence of God]; it will be only five or six printed sheets, but I hope it will contain a good part of my metaphysics."[55] Initially, Descartes had planned to send the manuscript to a few theologians for their comments.[56] He expanded the plan for objections and replies and sent the finished manuscript to Mersenne for distribution on November 11, 1640.[57]

At the time, when Mersenne was sending out the manuscript of the *Meditations*, Descartes thought himself at war with Scholastics, particularly with his old teachers, the Jesuits. He expected objections from them and thought he "must put himself in the proper posture to await them." For that reason, he told Mersenne that he felt like "reading some of their philosophy," something he said he had not done in twenty years, "to see whether it now seems to me better than I once thought." Thus, he requested Mersenne to send him "the names of authors who have written textbooks in philosophy and who have the most following among the Jesuits, and whether there are new ones from twenty years ago." Descartes, reminiscing about the Jesuit textbook authors he had known at La Flèche, then said he remembered only those of the Coimbran Jesuits, Franciscus Toletus, and Antonio Rubius, but also requested from Mersenne to tell him "Whether

---

Archiv für Geschichte der Philosophie 92 (2010): 290–303 (the quoted passage is on p. 295). The order of presentation of the printed *Meditations* starts with the Letter to the Doctors of the Sorbonne and follows with the (revised) Preface to the Reader, then the Synopsis of the Meditations. The text of the *Meditations* is next, with the *Objections* and *Replies* following directly after that.

54. Descartes to Mersenne (July 27, 1638), AT II, 267.

55. Descartes to Mersenne [November 13, 1639], AT II, 622.

56. Descartes to Mersenne [November 13, 1639], AT II, 622: "In order to improve it, I plan to have only twenty or thirty copies printed, to send them to twenty or thirty most learned theologians with whom I might be acquainted, in order to have their judgment of it and learn what should be changed, corrected, or added, before making it public."

57. Descartes to Mersenne [November 11, 1640], AT III, 238–40. See also Descartes to Mersenne (September 30, 1640), AT III, 183–85; Descartes to [Huygens] [November 11, 1640], AT III, 762; Descartes to Mersenne (November 11, 1640), AT III, 235–36; and Descartes to [Gibieuf] [November 11, 1640], AT III, 237–38.

there is someone who wrote a summary of all of Scholastic philosophy and who has a following, for this would spare me the time to read all their heavy tomes." Descartes recalled: "It seems to me that there was a Carthusian or a Feuillant who had accomplished this, but I do not remember his name."[58] Presumably, Mersenne identified Eustachius a Sancto Paulo as the Cistercian monk or Feuillant Descartes remembered having written a summary of all Scholastic philosophy in one volume, since, in his next letter to Mersenne, Descartes wrote: "I purchased the *Philosophy* of Brother Eustachius a Sancto Paulo," and added that Eustachius's *Summa* seems to him to be "the best book ever written on this matter."[59] Descartes continued to look for other Scholastic textbooks, seeking one as excellent as Eustachius's but written by a Jesuit. Not finding any, he settled on Eustachius's *Summa* as a book to use as a contrast for his philosophy. He initiated a new project, the precursor to the *Principles of Philosophy*:

> My intent is to write in sequence a textbook of my philosophy in the form of theses, in which, without any superfluity of discourse, I will place only my conclusions, together with the true reasons from which I draw them—what I think I can do in a few words. And in the same book, I will publish an ordinary philosophy text, such as perhaps that of Brother Eustachius, with my notes at the end of each question, to which I will add the various opinions of others and what one should believe about all of them, and perhaps, at the end, I will draw some comparisons between these two philosophies.[60]

A month later, Descartes informed Mersenne that he had begun the project. He soon abandoned it as a commentary on Eustachius, although he continued it as something he initially called *A Summary of Philosophy*; it then turned into the *Principles of Philosophy* and was published in 1644:[61]

---

58. Descartes to Mersenne (September 30, 1640), AT III, 184–85.
59. Descartes to Mersenne (November 11, 1640), AT III, 232.
60. Descartes to Mersenne (November 11, 1640), AT III, 233.
61. Descartes said to Mersenne, "I am unhappy to hear about the death of Father Eustachius; for, although this gives me greater freedom to write my notes on his philosophy, I would nevertheless have preferred to do this with his permission, while he was still alive" [January 21, 1641], AT III, 286.

Perhaps these scholastic wars will cause that my *World* will soon be seen by the world, and I believe it would be seen by now, except that I first want to teach it to speak Latin; and I will have it called *Summa Philosophiæ*, so that it is introduced more easily into the conversation of School people, Ministers as well as Jesuits, who currently persecute it and try to smother it before its birth.[62]

The *Principles of Philosophy* was thus a summary of Descartes's philosophy, starting with a rewritten and expanded version of his metaphysics in Part I and *The World* (speaking Latin), also rewritten and expanded, in Parts II through IV.

The question still to be answered is: What changed such that Descartes could bring *The World* into the world, whether speaking Latin or French (and now as a straightforward philosophy treatise, that is, no longer a fable)? The political-theological situation did not seem to have altered much, but Descartes made a myriad of modifications to the doctrines of *The World*, none so important for this purpose than his reworking of the definition of motion. This started with *Principles*, Part II, articles 24 and 25. Descartes asserted in article 24, about motion commonly speaking, that local motion, "in the vulgar sense, is nothing more than the action by which a body passes from one place to another," and added that since "the same thing may be said to change and not to change its place at the same time, we can say that it moves and does not move at the same time." The topic of article 25, about motion properly speaking, concerned the truth of the matter, not common parlance, and defined motion as "the transference of one part of matter or one body from the vicinity of those bodies in immediate contact with it, and regarded as at rest, into the vicinity of others."[63] These definitions were put to work in a discussion of the hypotheses used by Ptolemy, Copernicus, Tycho, and Descartes himself, in *Principles*, Part III, articles 15–19. Descartes rejected Ptolemy's hypothesis as "not in conformity with appearances," argued that "those of Copernicus and Tycho do not differ if considered only as hypotheses"; he asserted that "Tycho verbally attributes less motion to the earth than does Copernicus, but in fact attributes more to it." The crux of this dis-

---

62. Descartes to Huygens (January 31, 1642), AT III, 782.
63. See also *Principles*, Part II, articles 26–33, with reworked laws of motion in articles 36–53.

cussion happened in Part III, article 19, where Descartes claimed that he denied "the motion of the earth more carefully than Copernicus and more truthfully that Tycho." Descartes further concluded, in article 28, that "the earth does not move, properly speaking, and neither do any of the planets, although they are carried along by the heavens." He stated as well, in article 29, that "no motion is to be attributed to the earth, even if motion is taken improperly, in common parlance."[64] Thus, Descartes did not affirm the condemned proposition: for Descartes, the earth does not itself move but is carried by its heaven, which of course is moving. For good measure, he insisted that his accounts were hypothetical and that he assumed some "hypotheses, which it is certain are false."[65] Ultimately, in the last article of the *Principles*, Descartes piously affirmed that he submits all his opinions to the authority of the church: "At the same time, recalling my insignificance, I affirm nothing, but submit all these things to the authority of the Catholic Church and to the judgment of those wiser than myself; and I wish no one to believe anything I have written, unless he is personally persuaded by the force and evidence of reason."[66]

In between, Descartes recounted the doctrines of *The World* and added new hypothetical accounts of sunspots,[67] as well as novas and the formation of planets and comets from stars.[68] He then used these hypotheses to explain the formation of the earth from a sun whose sunspots have congealed and cooled to form a crust.[69] He also provided an extended explanation of the magnet and the magnetic force of the earth.[70] While these accounts looked new, as compared with those found in *The World*, we cannot be certain of this: there are chapters missing in what we have

---

64. Descartes added, that in the improper sense of motion, "it would be correct to say that the other planets move," and continued, in article 30, by asserting that "all the planets are carried around by the heavens." Article 33 explained that "the earth turns on its axis."
65. *Principles*, Part III, article 45. See also articles 46–47.
66. *Principles*, Part IV, article 207.
67. *Principles*, Part III, articles 72–110.
68. *Principles*, Part III, articles 111–18 and 119–26.
69. *Principles*, Part IV, articles 1–18, and 20–48 for the formation of water and air. After his explanation of the tides, in articles 49–56, Descartes returns to the nature of the earth and the various materials of which it is composed, articles 57–76; the causes of earthquakes, articles 77–79; and then nature of fire, articles 80–122; and the effects of fire, including an account of the formation and nature of glass, articles 123–32.
70. *Principles*, Part IV, articles 133–87.

of *The World* and *Man*.⁷¹ We do know that some materials were detached from *The World* and published separately as *Dioptrics* and *Meteors*.⁷² We can also see that the summary of the contents of *The World*, in *Discourse*, Part V, did not correspond very well with what survived of *The World*. The following passage from the *Discourse* fits better with what Descartes wrote in the *Principles* than with the contents of *The World* as it has come down to us:

> I went on to speak in particular about the earth: [. . .] how mountains, seas, springs and rivers could be formed there naturally, and metals could be found in mines, and plants grow in the fields, and generally how all the bodies called mixed or composite could be engendered there. And, among other things, because other than the stars I know of nothing else in the world except fire that produces light, I tried to make everything belonging to its nature clearly understood: how it is made, how it is nourished, how it sometimes has heat without light, and sometimes light without heat; how it can introduce various colors and various other qualities into various bodies; how it melts some and hardens others; how it can consume almost all of them or convert them into ashes and smoke; and finally how from these ashes, by the sheer force of its action, it produces glass—I took particular pleasure in describing this transmutation of ashes into glass because it seemed to me to be as admirable as any taking place in nature.⁷³

None of the materials about the earth survive as part of *The World*; its chapters about light discuss only the motion of light, not the production of colors or the production of ashes and their transmutation into glass.

But the greatest difference between the two works was that the contents of *Man* were almost completely missing from the *Principles*. In the

---

71. According to Claude Clerselier, *Man* was chapter 18 of *The World*, the manuscript of which, as he received it, was composed of fifteen chapters, that is, missing chapters 16 and 17 forming the transition between the two.

72. Perhaps *Dioptrics*, Discourse 1 and 2, about light and refraction. Discourses 3 through 8, about the eye and vision, clearly overlap the materials in various sections of *Man*. *Meteors*, Discourse 8 through 10, about the rainbow, coronas, and false suns were probably also included in *The World*; Discourse 1 through 7 (about the nature of terrestrial bodies, vapors and exhalations, salt, winds, clouds, snow, rain and hail, and storms and lightning) are also candidates for sections that might originally have been in *The World*.

73. *Discourse on Method*, V, AT VI, 44–45 (see Appendix B).

Discourse, Descartes described the transition from the chapters that constituted *The World* to those that constituted *Man* as follows:

> From the description of inanimate bodies and plants, I passed to that of animals and, in particular, to that of men. But I did not yet have sufficient knowledge to speak of them in the same manner as I did the rest, that is, by demonstrating effects from causes and showing what seeds and in what manner nature must produce them. Thus, I contented myself with supposing that God formed the body of a man exactly like one of ours, as much in the external shape of its members as in the internal arrangement of its organs, composing it only out of the matter I had described and at the beginning without putting into it any rational soul, or anything else to serve as a vegetative or sensitive soul, but rather that he kindled in its heart one of these fires without light I had already explained.[74]

In the *Principles*, Descartes clarified that he previously intended to write two other parts to the *Principles*, a Part V on living things, that is, on animals and plants, and a Part VI on man. He asserted that he was not clear about all the matters in them and was not able to make the necessary experiments to complete them. He then continued with the only material from *Man* that he inserted in the *Principles*, that is, a discussion of the object of the senses, "in order not to delay these earlier parts too long or to allow anything to be missing which I should have reserved for the others"; as he explained:

> Up to this point I have described the earth and all the visible world as if it were simply a machine in which there was nothing to consider but the shape and motion of its parts, and yet our senses cause other things to be presented to us, such as colors, smells, sounds, and other such things; if I did not speak of them, it might be thought that I had omitted the main part of the explanation of the things in nature.[75]

---

74. *Discourse on Method*, V, AT VI, 45–46 (see Appendix B).
75. *Principles*, Part IV, article 188. A discussion of sensation follows: the different kinds of sensation, internal sensations, that is, passions or emotions and natural appetites, and the external senses—touch, taste, smell, hearing, and sight (articles 189–95). These are then succeeded by articles asserting: that the soul does not feel except insofar as the thing is in the brain; the mind is of such a nature that from the motion of the body alone, various

Three years later, in the Preface to the French translation of the *Principles*, Descartes reiterated his intention to complete the missing Parts V and VI and his claim that he was not able to do so for lack of sufficient experiments:

> I believe myself to have begun to explain the whole of philosophy. [. . .] To carry this plan to a conclusion, I should afterward in the same way explain in further detail the nature of each of the other bodies on the earth, that is, minerals, plants, animals, and above all man, then finally treat exactly of medicine, morals, and mechanics. All this I should have to do in order to give to mankind a complete body of philosophy; I do not feel myself to be so old, I do not so much despair of my strength, and I do not find myself so far removed from a knowledge of what remains that I should not venture to endeavor to achieve this design, if I had the means of making all the experiments I would need in order to support and justify my reasoning.[76]

Descartes did, in fact, continue working on Parts V and VI of the *Principles*, trying to finish his accounts of animals and reworking the parts of *Man* he found problematic. There is an unfinished manuscript called the *Description of the Human Body* among the papers left behind in Stockholm after his death on February 11, 1650.[77] The first three parts of the treatise contain rewritten sections from *Man* on the motion of the heart and blood and on nutrition, but Parts IV and V contain new materials on the formation of the fetus. Descartes announced these materials as follows:

> We can acquire a still more perfect knowledge of the way all parts of the body are nourished if we consider how they were originally produced in the seed. Until now I did not want to put my opinions on this topic in writing because I had not yet performed enough experiments to verify by means of them all the thoughts I had on this matter. Nevertheless, I cannot refrain from setting out here in passing some very general

---

sensations can be excited in it; there is nothing known of external objects by the senses but their shape, size, or motion; and there is no phenomenon in nature that has not been dealt with in this treatise (articles 196–99).

76. *Principles*, AT IXb, 16–17.

77. AT XI, 223–86 (see Appendix C for a summary of the contents of the *Description of the Human Body*).

thoughts which I hope are those least likely to be among the ones I will have to retract later, when new experiments will have enlightened me further.⁷⁸

It is not difficult to see that the *Description of the Human Body* was at least the start of a portion of the missing *Principles*, Part V on animals. Similarly, the *Passions of the Soul*, which Descartes published a few months before he died, can be seen as a portion of the missing Part VI of the *Principles*, on man.⁷⁹ Thus, *The World* was reborn as *Principles of Philosophy* and Descartes continued to work on *Man*. In the meanwhile, copies of *The World* and *Man* were circulating in manuscript form.⁸⁰

The World was first published posthumously as *Le Monde de Mr. Descartes ou le Traité de la Lumière* (Paris, 1664), and *Man* first appeared two years earlier, in Latin translation by Florentino Schuyl, as *Renatus Descartes de Homine* (Leyden, 1662). Claude Clerselier, who had access to Descartes's original manuscripts, brought out a French edition of *Man*, *L'Homme de René Descartes* (Paris, 1664), and a revised edition of both texts, *L'Homme de René Descartes. [. . .] A quoi on ajouté Le Monde ou Traité de la lumière du mesme auteur* (Paris, 1677).⁸¹ This publication history itself clearly indicates that copies of *The World* and *Man* were in circulation independently of Descartes since the manuscripts he had in Stockholm were sent to

---

78. AT XI, 252–53.

79. The *Treatise on Man*, as we have it, is clearly incomplete. Descartes asserts numerous times that people are composed of a soul and a body, that he will first describe the body by itself, and afterward the soul, also by itself, and finally, that he will show how these two natures should be joined and united to compose people resembling us; but he never really gets to the second or third steps. *Passions of the Soul* begins with a summary of *Man* and goes on to give an account of the passions in terms of the psycho-physical union of mind and body.

80. In fact, a previously unknown translation of the *Treatise on Man* was recently found at the Leiden University Libraries by Erik-Jan Bos, who is preparing the publication of the Latin manuscript.

81. The texts of *Le Monde* and *L'Homme* are given in the standard edition of the *Works* of Descartes (AT) vol. XI. AT follows the Clerselier 1677 edition, with variants from some of the previous editions indicated in the footnotes. The figures are not Descartes's own, although those in *The World* are based on sketches, no longer extant, by Descartes. Clerselier commissioned his own figures for *Man*, which are reproduced here and are considerably different from those used by Schuyl, who tried to provide some more realistic anatomical illustrations.

Clerselier in Paris after his death, and *The World* and *Man* were first published by editors other than Clerselier. In fact, Descartes had indicated that he had loaned the manuscript of *Man* to some friends for them to copy; in a letter to Mersenne from November 23, 1646, he said: "It was already twelve or thirteen years since I described all the functions of the human or animal body, but the paper on which I wrote it is so scribbled up that I would myself have much trouble reading it; however, I could not refrain, four or five years ago, from loaning it to a close friend who made a copy of it, which was since transcribed again by two others, with my permission, but without my rereading or correcting them."[82] Thus there were at least three independent copies circulating, likely more.

The influence of the publication of *Man* cannot be overstated.[83] Nicolas Malebranche's early biographer, Yves André, recounted a story about Malebranche, who was walking in Paris in 1664 and stopped to ask a bookseller whether there were any new books. Clerselier had just published *Man*, which the bookseller showed Malebranche. Although inclined against Descartes, Malebranche leafed through the book, found it very sensible, admired its method, and bought it. André said that Malebranche discovered truths in the book so luminous, deduced in such a marvelous, divine order, that Malebranche became ecstatic: the joys of learning so many new discoveries caused him violent heart palpitations. Consequently, Malebranche undertook a ten-year study of Descartes's works, which yielded his magnum opus, *The Search after Truth*, in

---

82. Descartes to Mersenne (November 23, 1646), AT IV, 566–67. The context of the statement is interesting; it occurs when Descartes was complaining about Henricus Regius having gotten a hold of a copy of *Man* and using it for his own purposes: "And I begged them not to show it to anyone, as I also never wanted to have it shown to Regius since I knew his disposition and, thinking I would publish my opinions on this matter, I did not desire anyone else to take away the virtue of novelty. But he got a copy of this text despite me, without my being able in any way to figure out how he got it, and he pulled from it this nice piece on the motion of the muscles" (AT IV, 567). Descartes claimed that Regius misunderstood the argument about the muscles because the copy he got was missing the figures. See Descartes to Mersenne (October 5, 1646), AT IV, 510–11, Descartes to [Colvius?] [October 5, 1646], AT IV, 517–18, and Descartes to Elisabeth [March 1647], AT IV, 625–27. We can surmise that three friends with copies of the manuscript were Alphonse Pollot, Anthonis Studler van Surck, and Adriaan Heereboord; it is possible that Pollot made a copy for Princess Elisabeth who might have shared it with Regius.

83. *The World*, of course, was available in some fashion as part of the *Principles of Philosophy* and was most influential in that way as well.

1674–1675.[84] In the eighteenth century, thinkers such as Julien Offray de La Mettrie wrote works such as *Man a Machine* (1748), that were both deeply indebted and deeply critical of Descartes's *Man*.[85]

---

84. Yves Marie André, *La vie du R. P. Malebranche* (1886; repr. Geneva: Slatkin Reprints, 1970), 11–12.

85. For more on the reception of Descartes's *Man*, see the various essays in *Descartes'* Treatise on Man *and its Reception*, ed. Delphine-Antoine Mahut and Stephen Gaukroger (Cham, Switzerland: Springer, 2016). I would like to express my gratitude to Erik-Jan Bos, my collaborator on many Descartes projects, for his invaluable assistance on this project, and my admiration for his superb work on Descartes.

Part I

The World or Treatise on Light

Chapter 1. The Difference between Our Sensations and the Things That Produce Them[1]

In proposing to treat here the subject of light, the first thing I want to call your attention to is that there can be a difference between the sensation we have of light, that is, the idea formed of it in our imagination through the intermediary of our eyes and what is in the objects producing this sensation in us, that is, what is in the flame or in the sun called by the name of light. For even though everyone is commonly persuaded that the ideas we have in our thought are completely like the objects from which they proceed, nevertheless, I do not see any reason assuring us that this is so. I note, on the contrary, many experiences that should make us doubt it.

As you well know, words have no resemblance to the things they signify, yet they do not fail to make us conceive of them, often even when we are not paying attention to the sound of the words or to their syllables. It can happen, in this way, that after we heard a discourse whose meaning we understood very well, we might not be able to say in what language it was spoken. Now, if words, which signify nothing except by human convention, suffice to make us conceive of things to which they bear no resemblance, why could not nature have established a certain sign that makes us have the sensation of light, even though that sign does not in itself have anything like that sensation? Is it not thus that nature established laughter and tears, so that we may read joy and sadness on the face of people?

But perhaps you will say that our ears allow us to sense truly only the sounds of the words, and our eyes only the countenance of the person who laughs or cries, and it is our mind which, having retained what those words and that countenance signify, represents the meaning to us at the

---

1. We are following the text of the 1677 edition and will be indicating the chapter titles as given in the 1664 edition in the footnotes.

same time. I could reply that, all the same, it is our mind which represents to us the idea of light each time the action signifying it touches our eye. But without wasting time debating this matter, I would rather bring forward another example.

Do you think that, even when we are not paying attention to the meaning of words and hear only their sound, the idea of this sound formed in our thought is something like the object which is its cause? A person opens his mouth, moves his tongue, pushes out his breath—in all these actions I see nothing that is not very different from the idea of sound they make us imagine. Most philosophers assure us that sound is nothing other than a certain vibration of air striking our ears. Thus, if the sense of hearing related the true image of its object to our thought, it had to make us conceive the motion of the parts of air then vibrating against our ears, instead of making us conceive of the sound. But perhaps not everyone will want to believe what the philosophers say, so I will bring forward another example.

Of all our senses, touch is the one considered the least deceptive and the most certain; so, if I show you that even touch makes us conceive of several ideas in no way resembling the objects producing them, I do not think you should find it strange if I say that sight can do the same. Now there is no one who does not know that the ideas of tickling and of pain, formed in our thought on the occasion of our being touched by external bodies, bear no resemblance to those sensations. You pass a feather lightly over the lips of a child falling asleep, and he senses that he is being tickled. Do you think the idea of tickling he conceives resembles something which is in this feather? A soldier returns from combat; during the heat of battle, he could have been wounded without perceiving it. But now that he is beginning to cool off, he senses some pain and believes he was wounded. A surgeon is called, his armor is removed, and he is examined. In the end it is discovered that what he was sensing was nothing but a buckle or a strap caught under his armor, which was pressing on him and making him feel uncomfortable. If his sense of touch, in making him feel this strap, had impressed its image on his thought, there would have been no need of a surgeon to tell him what he was sensing.

Now, I see no reason requiring us to believe that what is in the objects from which the sensation of light comes to us is any more like that sensation than the actions of a feather or a strap are to tickling and pain. And yet I did not bring forward these examples to make you believe absolutely that this light is different in the objects and in our eyes, but only so that you might feel doubtful about this matter and could keep yourself from being preoccupied with the contrary, and you can now better examine with me what light is.

Chapter 2. What the Heat and Light of Fire Consists of[2]

I know of only two sorts of bodies in the world in which light is found, namely, the stars and flame or fire. And because the stars are no doubt less accessible to human knowledge than fire or a flame, I will first try to explain what I observe regarding the flame.

When a flame burns wood or some other similar material, we can see with our eyes that it moves the small parts of the wood and separates them from one another, thus transforming the subtlest parts into fire, air, or smoke, and leaving the coarsest parts as ashes. Someone else may, if he wishes, imagine in this wood the form of fire, the quality of heat, and the action that burns, as completely different things; in my case, since I am afraid of making a mistake by assuming something more than I see must necessarily be there, I am satisfied in conceiving of the motion of its parts. For put fire and heat in the wood and make the wood burn as much as you please, if you do not also suppose that any of its parts can move and detach itself from its neighboring parts, I could not imagine that it undergoes any alteration or change. In contrast, remove the fire, remove the heat, prevent the wood from burning, as long as you grant me only that there is some power putting the subtler parts into violent motion and separating them from the coarser ones, I find that this alone will be able to bring about all the changes in the wood we experience when it burns.

Now, since it does not seem possible to conceive that a body can move another unless it itself is also moving, I conclude, as a result, that the body of the flame acting against the wood is composed of small parts moving independently of one another by very rapid and very violent motions. Moving in this way, they push and move with them the parts of the bodies they touch and those not offering them too much resistance. I say that its parts move independently of one another because, although several of them often work together and conspire to produce a single effect, we see, nevertheless, each of them acting on its own against the bodies they touch.

---

2. 1664 edition title: What It Is to Burn, Heat, and Illuminate in Fire.

I say also that their motion is very rapid and very violent because, since they are so small that we cannot distinguish them by sight, they could not have enough force to act against the other bodies, if the rapidity of their motion did not compensate for their lack of size.

I add nothing about the direction in which each part moves. For if you consider that the power to move and the power to determine in what direction the motion must take place are two completely different things, of which one can exist without the other (as I explained in the *Dioptrics*),[3] you can easily judge that each one moves in the manner made less difficult by the disposition of the bodies surrounding it. In the same flame there may be parts going up and others going down in straight lines, and in circles, and from all sides, without it changing anything of its nature. As a result, if you see almost all of them tending upward, you must not think that this is for any other reason except that the other bodies touching them are almost always disposed to offer them more resistance in all the other directions.

But having recognized that the parts of the flame move in this manner, and that, to understand how it has the power to consume the wood and to burn it suffices to conceive of their motions, let us please examine whether the same would not also suffice to make us understand how the flame heats and illuminates us. For if we can discover this, it will no longer be necessary for the flame to have any other quality, and we could say that it is motion alone which is sometimes called heat and sometimes called light, according to the different effects it produces.

With respect to heat, I think, the sensation we have of it can be taken for a kind of pain, when it is violent, and sometimes for a kind of tickling, when it is a moderate. And since we said there is nothing outside our thought similar to the ideas we conceive of in respect to tickling and pain, we can well believe also that there is nothing similar to the one we conceive of with respect to heat; rather, anything that can move differentially the small parts of our hands, or of some other place in our body, can arouse this sensation in us. This view is even supported by several observations. For we can heat our hands merely by rubbing them together, and any other body can also be heated without being placed in contact with a fire, provided only that it is agitated and shaken in such a way that many of its small parts are moved and can thus move the small parts of our hands.

---

3. See AT VI, 94 and 97.

With respect to light, we can also conceive that the same motion in the flame suffices to make us sense it. But because the principal part of my project consists in this, I want to try to explain it at some length and to resume my discussion from before.

Chapter 3. Hardness and Liquidity[4]

I consider that there is an infinity of various motions enduring perpetually in the world. And after having noted the greatest of these, causing the days, months, and years, I take note that the vapors of the earth never cease to rise toward the clouds and descend from them, the air is always agitated by winds, the sea is never at rest, springs and rivers flow ceaselessly, the firmest buildings finally fall into decay, plants and animals either grow or deteriorate; in short, there is nothing anywhere not changing. As a result, I know clearly that the flame is not alone in having many small parts continually moving, but all other bodies have such parts, although their actions are not as violent, and they cannot be perceived by any of our senses because of their smallness.

I do not stop to look for the cause of their motion, for it is sufficient for me to think that they began to move as soon as the world began to exist. And that being so, I find based on my reasons, that it is impossible for their motions ever to cease or even for them to change in any way other than with respect to their subject. That is, the virtue or power of a body to move itself may well pass wholly or partially to another body, and thus no longer be in the former, but it cannot no longer exist in the world. My reasons, I say, are sufficient to satisfy me on this point; but I did not yet have the occasion to relate them to you. In the meanwhile, you can imagine, if you see fit, as do most of the learned, that there is some prime mover, which, rolling around the world at an incomprehensible speed, is the origin and source of all the other motions found in it.

Now, following from this consideration, there is a way of explaining the cause of all the changes taking place in the world and of all the varieties appearing on the earth; but I will limit myself here to speaking of those useful for my topic.

---

4. 1664 edition title: Where We See the Variety, Duration, and Cause of Motion, with the Explanation of the Hardness and Liquidity of Bodies in Which It Is Found.

The difference between hard bodies and liquid ones is the first one I want you to note, and for this purpose, consider that each body can be divided into extremely small parts. I do not want to determine whether their number is infinite or not; but at least it is certain that, with respect to our knowledge, it is indefinite, and we can suppose that there are several millions of them in the smallest grain of sand our eyes can perceive.

And note that, if two of these small parts touch one another, without being in the act of moving away from one another, some force is needed to separate them, however small it may be; for once they are so positioned, they would never be inclined to dispose themselves differently. Note also that it takes twice as much force to separate two of them as it does to separate one, and a thousand times as much to separate a thousand of them. Thus, if we had to separate several millions of them at the same time, as may be needed to break a single hair, it is no wonder if a rather significant force is required.

On the other hand, if two or more of these small parts touch one another only in passing, and when they are in the act of moving, one in one direction, the other in another, it is certain that less force will be needed to separate them than if they were completely without motion; and indeed, no force at all will be required, if the motion with which they can separate themselves is equal to or greater than the one with which we want to separate them.

Now I find no other difference between hard and liquid bodies, except that the parts of the ones can be separated from the whole much more easily than those of others. Thus, to constitute the hardest body imaginable, I think it suffices if all its parts touch, without any space remaining between any two, nor any of them being in the act of moving. For what glue or what cement can be imagined there, beyond this, to have them hold one another better?

I also think that, to constitute the most liquid body that can be found, it is enough if all its smallest parts are moving away from one another in the most diverse ways and as quickly as possible, even though they do not cease being able to touch each other on all sides, and to arrange themselves in as small a space, as if they were without motion. Finally, I believe that each body approaches these two extremities more or less, according to whether its parts are more or less in the act of moving away from one another. And all the observations upon which I cast my eyes confirm me in this opinion.

Flame, whose parts I already said are all perpetually agitated, is not only liquid, but it also renders most other bodies liquid. And note that when it melts metals, it acts with no different power than when it burns wood. But, because the parts of metals are all approximately equal, it cannot move one part without moving the other, and thus it forms completely liquid bodies from them. In contrast, the parts of wood are so unequal that it can separate the smaller parts and render them liquid, that is, make them fly away in smoke, without thus agitating the larger parts.

After flame, there is nothing more liquid than air, and one can see with the naked eye that its parts move separately from one another. For if you deign to observe these small bodies commonly called atoms that appear in rays of sunlight, you will see them fluttering incessantly here and there in a thousand different ways, even when there is no wind agitating them. You can also experience the same kind of thing in all the coarsest liquids if you mix them together in different colors, so as to better distinguish their motions. And finally, this appears very clearly in acids when they move and separate the parts of some metal.

But at this point, you could ask, if it is solely the motion of the parts of the flame that causes it to burn and make it liquid, why the motion of the parts of the air, which also renders it extremely liquid, does not all give it the same power to burn, but on the contrary, makes it such that our hands can hardly feel it? To this I reply that we must not only take into account the speed of motion, but also the size of the parts; the smaller ones make the more liquid bodies, but the larger ones have more force to burn, and in general to act on other bodies.

Note in passing, that I take here and from now on will take a single part to be everything joined together and not in the act of separating, even though the parts, however small they may be, could easily be divided into many other smaller parts. Thus, a grain of sand, a stone, a rock, and the whole earth itself, may from now on be taken as a single part, insofar as we are considering here only a completely simple and equal motion.

Now if, among the parts of the air, there are some very large ones in comparison with others, as are the atoms seen there, they also move very slowly; and if there are some moving more quickly, they are also smaller. But if, among the parts of the flame, there are some smaller than in air, there are also larger ones, or at least there are a larger number of parts of the same size as the largest parts of the air, and they move much more quickly; and it is only these latter ones that have the power to burn.

That there are smaller parts may be conjectured by their penetrating many bodies whose pores are so narrow that even air cannot enter. That there are larger parts, or parts as large but in greater numbers, we can see clearly in that air alone is not enough to nourish the flame. That they move more quickly is experienced well enough by the violence of their action. And finally, that the largest of these parts and not the others have the power to burn, is apparent in that the flame issuing out from brandy, or from other very subtle bodies, hardly burns at all, while on the contrary, the one engendered in hard and heavy bodies is very hot.

Chapter 4. The Void, and How It Happens That Our Senses Do Not Perceive Certain Bodies[5]

But we must examine more specifically why the air, even though it is a body as any other, cannot be sensed as well as they are sensed. In this way, we will free ourselves from an error we were all concerned about from our childhood, when we believed there were no other bodies around us than those that could be sensed, and thus, if air was one of these, because we sensed it faintly, it should not at least be as material and solid as those we sensed more clearly.

Regarding this, I would first want you to notice that all bodies, both hard and liquid, are made of the same matter, and it is impossible to conceive of the parts of this matter ever composing a more solid body, or one occupying less space, than they do when each of them is touched on all sides by the others surrounding it. As a result, it seems to me that, if there can be a void anywhere, it must be in hard bodies rather than in liquid ones; for it is evident that the parts of the latter can much more easily press and arrange against one another, because they are moving, than can those of the former, which are without motion.

For example, if you put some powder in a jar, you shake the jar and pound against it to make room for more powder; but if you pour some liquid into it, it immediately arranges itself in as small a place it can be put. Indeed, if you consider on this subject some of the observations philosophers commonly use to show that there is no void in nature, you will easily recognize that all these spaces people consider empty, and where we

---

5. 1664 edition title: What Judgment We Should Make about the Void, and Why Our Senses Do Not Perceive Some Bodies.

sense only air, are at least as full, and as full of the same matter, as those where we sense other bodies.

For please tell me what is the likelihood that nature would cause the heaviest bodies to rise and the most solid to break, as one experiences nature doing in certain machines, rather than suffer any of their parts to stop touching one another, or to touch some other bodies, and yet allow the parts of air, which are so easy to bend and be arranged in all manners, to remain next to one another without being touched on all sides, or even without there being another body among them that they touch? Could one really believe that the water in a well must rise upward against its natural inclination merely so that the pipe of a pump may be filled and also think that the water in the clouds should not fall to try to fill the spaces here below, if there were even a slight void among the parts of the bodies they contain?

But you could propose to me a rather considerable difficulty here, namely, that the parts composing liquid bodies cannot, it seems, move incessantly, as I said they do, unless there is some empty space among them, at least in the places from which they depart as they move. I would have difficulty answering this, had I not recognized by various observations that all the motions in the world are in some way circular. That is, when a body leaves its place, it always comes into that of another body, and that other body into that of another, and that other into another still, and so on until the last body at the same instant occupies the place vacated by the first. Thus, there is no more of a void among bodies when they are moving than when they are at rest. And note here, for this to happen, it is not necessary that all the parts of the bodies moving together be exactly disposed around as in a true circle, or even that they be of the same size and shape, for these inequalities can easily be compensated for by other inequalities in their speeds.

We do not usually notice these circular motions when bodies move in the air, because we are accustomed to conceiving of the air only as an empty space. But look at the fish swimming in the basin of a fountain. If they do not get too near the surface of the water, they will not make the surface move at all, even though they pass underneath it with great speed. From this it plainly appears that the water the fish push before them does not push indifferently all the water of the basin but pushes only the water that can better serve in perfecting the circle of their motion and can come into the place they abandon.

This observation suffices to show how these circular motions are easy and familiar in nature. But I now wish to relate another one to show that there is never any motion which is not circular. When the wine in a cask does not flow through an opening at the bottom because the top is completely closed, it is improper to say, as is ordinarily done, that this takes place because of fear of the void. We know well that the wine does not have a mind to fear anything; and even if it did, I do not know what reason it could have to be apprehensive of that void, which is in fact nothing but a chimera. Rather, we must say that it cannot leave the cask because outside everything is as full as it can be, and the part of the air whose place it would occupy, if it were to flow out, cannot find another place to occupy in the rest of the universe, unless an opening were made at the top of the cask through which this air can rise by a circular path into its place.

However, I do not wish to say for certain that there is no void at all in nature. I fear that my treatise would become too long if I undertook to explain the matter at length, and the observations I spoke of are not sufficient to prove it, although they are sufficient to persuade us that the spaces in which we sense nothing are filled with the same matter, and contain at least as much of that matter, as those occupied by bodies we sense. Thus, for example, when a vessel is full of gold or lead, it contains no more matter than when we think it is empty. This may seem very strange to many whose reason does not extend beyond their fingertips and who think there is nothing in the world except what they touch. But when you have considered a little what makes us sense or not sense a body, I am certain you will find nothing incredible in this. For you will obviously recognize that, far from all the things around us being able to be sensed, on the contrary, those there most frequently can be sensed the least, and those always there can never be sensed.

The heat of our heart is very great, but we do not sense it, because it is ordinary. The weight of our body is not small, but it does not discomfort us. We do not even sense the weight of our clothes, because we are accustomed to wearing them. The reason for this is clear enough: for it is certain that we cannot sense any body, unless it is the cause of some change in our sensory organs, that is, unless it moves in some way the small parts of the matter of which these organs are composed. The objects not always presenting themselves can well do this well enough, provided only that they have enough force; for, if they corrupt something there while they are acting, it can be repaired afterward by nature when they are no longer acting. But if those continually touching us ever had the power to produce any change in our senses, and to move any parts of their matter, by dint of moving them they must have had the power to separate them entirely from the others at the beginning of our life; and thus, they can only have left those that completely resist their action, and by means of which they cannot be sensed in any way. Thus, you see it is no wonder that there are many spaces around us in which we do not sense any body, although they contain bodies no less than those spaces in which we sense them the most.

But we must not think, as a result, that this coarse air we draw into our lungs while breathing, which is converted into wind when agitated, seems solid when enclosed in a balloon, and is composed only of exhalations and fumes, is as solid as water or earth. We must follow in this the common opinion of the philosophers who assure everyone that it is more rarefied. And this is easily recognized from experience: for the parts of a drop of water, separated from one another by the agitation of heat, can make up much more of this air than the space holding the water could contain. From this it follows indubitably that there is a great quantity of small intervals among the parts of which the air is composed; for there is no other way to conceive of a rare body. But because these intervals cannot be empty, as I said earlier, I conclude from all this that there are necessarily some other bodies, one or many, mixed with the air, filling the small intervals left among its parts as exactly as possible. It only remains now to consider what these other bodies can be; after this, I hope it will not be difficult to understand what the nature of light can be.

Chapter 5. The Number of Elements and Their Qualities[6]

The philosophers assure that there is above the clouds a certain air much more subtle than ours, which is not composed of the terrestrial vapors like our air but constitutes an element by itself. They also say that above this air there is yet another, much subtler body, they call the element of fire. They add moreover that these two elements are mixed with water and earth in the composition of all inferior bodies. Thus, I would only be following their opinion, if I said that this more subtle air and this element of fire fill the intervals among the parts of the coarser air we breathe, so that these

---

6. 1664 edition title: Reduction of the Four Elements to Three, with Their Explanation and Establishment.

bodies, interlaced with one another, compose a mass as solid as any body can be.

But so that I can better make you understand my thoughts on this subject, and so that you do not think I want to oblige you to believe everything the philosophers tell us about the elements, I must describe them to you in my fashion.

I conceive of the first, which can be called the element of fire, in the fashion of a liquid, the most subtle and most penetrating one in the world. And following from what was said before regarding the nature of liquid bodies, I imagine its parts to be much smaller and move much faster than any of the parts of other bodies. Or rather, in order not to be constrained to admit any void in nature, I do not attribute to it parts having no determined size or shape; but I am persuaded that the impetuosity of its movement is sufficient to cause it to be divided, in every way and every sense, by the collision with other bodies, and that its parts change shape at every moment to accommodate themselves to the shapes of the places they enter. Thus, there is never a passage so narrow, or an angle so small, among the parts of other bodies, into which the parts of this element do not penetrate without any difficulty, and do not exactly fill.

As for the second, which can be taken as the element of air, I also conceive of it as a very subtle liquid in comparison with the third; but in comparison with the first, there is need to attribute some size and shape to each of its parts, and to imagine them almost all round and joined together like grains of sand and dust. Thus, they cannot arrange themselves so well, or so press against each other that many small intervals do not always remain around them, into which it is much easier for the first element to slide than for parts of the second element to change shape expressly to fill them. And so, I am convinced that nowhere in the world can this second element be so pure that some small matter of the first is not always with it.

Beyond these two elements, I accept only a third, namely, that of earth. I judge its parts to be proportionally larger and move more slowly in comparison with those of the second as those of the second in comparison with those of the first. And I even believe that it is enough to conceive it as one or more large masses whose parts have very little or no motion that might cause them to change position with respect to one another.

If you find it strange that, to explain these elements, I do not make use of the qualities called hot, cold, moist, and dry, as do the philosophers, I will say to you that these qualities seem to me to require explanation.

And, unless I am mistaken, not only these four qualities, but also all others, and even all the forms of inanimate bodies, can be explained without needing to assume anything in their matter than the motion, size, shape, and arrangement of its parts. As a result, I will easily make you understand why I do not accept other elements than the three I described. For the difference between the three elements and the other bodies the philosophers call mixed, or varied and composite, consists in the forms of these mixed bodies always containing in themselves some qualities that oppose and counteract one another, or at least that do not tend to the conservation of one another. But the forms of the elements must be simple and must not have any qualities that do not accord so perfectly with one another that each tends to the conservation of all the others.

Now I could not find any such forms in the world except the three I described. For the form I attributed to the first element consists in its parts moving so extremely fast and being so small that there are no other bodies capable of stopping them; beyond that, they do not require any determinate size, shape, or position. The form of the second element consists in its parts having a motion and size so moderate that if there are several causes in the world that can increase their motion and decrease their size, there are just as many others that can do the opposite; and so, they always remain as it were in balance in this same moderate state. And the form of the third element consists in its parts being so large or so joined together that they always have the force to resist the motion of other bodies.

Examine as much as you want all the forms that can be given to mixed bodies by the various motions, the various shapes and sizes, the various arrangements of parts of matter. I am sure you would find none that does not in itself have qualities tending to make it change and, in changing, to reduce it to one of the forms of the elements.

Flame, for example, whose form requires its parts moving very fast, and in addition having some size, as was said earlier, cannot last long without being corrupted. For, either the size of its parts, in giving them the force to act against the other bodies, will be the cause of the diminution of their motion, or the violence of their agitation, in causing them to break by hurtling against the bodies they meet, will be the cause of their loss of size; and thus, little by little they will be able to be reduced to the form of the third element, or to that of the second, and even also some to that of the first. And in this way, you can understand the difference between this flame, or the fire common among us, and the element of fire I described.

You should also know that the elements of air and earth, that is, the second and third elements, are not like this coarse air we breathe, nor like this earth on which we are walking, but that, generally, all the bodies appearing around us are mixed or composite and subject to corruption.

And yet we need not therefore think the elements have no places in the world particularly intended for them, where they can be preserved perpetually in their natural purity. On the contrary, each part of matter always tends to be reduced to one of their forms and, once having been reduced, never tends to leave it. Even if God had created in the beginning only mixed bodies, nevertheless, since the world began, all these bodies would have had the opportunity to leave their forms and take on those of the elements. Thus, there is now great likelihood that all the bodies large enough to be counted among the most notable parts of the universe each have the form of only one of these elements, and there can be no mixed bodies anywhere, except on the surfaces of these large bodies. But there, it is necessary that there be some mixed bodies; for, the elements being of a very contrary nature, it cannot happen for two of them to touch each other without acting against each other's surfaces and thus imparting to the matter there the various forms of these mixed bodies.

Regarding this, if we generally consider all the bodies of which the universe is composed, we will find only three sorts that can be called large and counted among its main parts: namely, the sun and the fixed stars as the first, the heavens for the second, and the earth with the planets and the comets for the third. As a result, we have good reason to think that the sun and the fixed stars have no other form than that of the wholly pure first element, the heavens, that of the second, and the earth, with the planets and comets, that of the third.

I associate the planets and comets with the earth; for, seeing that they, like it, resist light and reflect its rays, I find no difference among these. I also associate the sun with the fixed stars, and attribute to them a nature quite contrary to that of the earth, for the action of their light alone is sufficient to let me know that their bodies are of a very subtle and very agitated matter.

As for the heavens, since they cannot be perceived by our senses, I think I am right to attribute to them a middle nature between that of the luminous bodies whose action we sense and that of the solid and heavy bodies whose resistance we sense.

Finally, we do not perceive any mixed body in any place other than on the surface of the earth; and if we consider that all the space containing them, that is, everything from the highest clouds to the deepest pits that people's greed ever dug up to mine its metals is extremely small in comparison with the earth and the immense expanses of the heaven, we can easily imagine that these mixed bodies are all together only like a crust generated on top of the earth by the agitation and the mixing of the matter of heaven surrounding it.

And thus, we will have occasion to think that it is not only in the air we breathe, but also all the other composite bodies, down to the hardest rocks and the heaviest metals, that there are parts of the element of air mixed with those of earth, and consequently also parts of the element of fire, because some of these are always found in the pores of the element of air.

But it should be noted that even though there are parts of these three elements mixed with one another in all these bodies, however, strictly speaking, only those which, because of their size or the difficulty they have in moving, can be referred to the third as making up all the bodies we see around us. For the parts of the other two elements are so subtle that they cannot be perceived by our senses. And we can represent all these bodies as we do sponges, in which, although there are in them many pores or small holes always full of air or water, or some similar liquid, these liquids, however, are not considered to be part of the composition of the sponge.

There are still many other things to explain here, and I would even be glad to add several reasons to make my opinions more plausible. But so that the length of this discourse will be less boring to you, I want to enclose part of it in the form of a fable, during which I hope that the truth will not fail to manifest itself sufficiently and will not be less pleasant to see than if I set it forth wholly naked.

Chapter 6. Description of a New World and the Qualities of the Matter of Which It Is Composed[7]

Allow your thought to wander outside this world for a little time, then, so that you may come to see another, wholly different world I will bring

---

7. 1664 edition title: Description of a New World, Which Is Very Easy to Grasp, but However It Is Like Ours, and Even Like the Chaos the Poets Imagined Having Preceded It.

into existence before you in imaginary spaces. The philosophers tell us that these spaces are infinite, and they certainly should be believed, since they themselves constructed them. But, in order to keep this infinity from bothering and embarrassing us, let us try not to go all the way to the end; let us enter it only far enough to lose from view all the creatures God made five or six thousand years ago and, after stopping there in some determinate place, let us suppose that God creates anew so much matter around us that, whatever direction our imagination can be extended, it no longer perceives any place that is void.

Even though the sea is not infinite, those in its midst on some vessel can extend their view to infinity, it seems, and nevertheless, there is still water beyond what they see. Thus, even though our imagination seems to be able to extend to infinity, and this new matter is not assumed to be infinite, we can still assume, all the same, that it fills up much greater spaces than all the ones we imagined. To ensure there is nothing in all this you might find objectionable, let us not allow our imagination to extend even as far as it could, but let us purposely confine it in a determinate space, one not greater, for example, than the distance from the earth to the principal stars of the firmament. And let us suppose that the matter God created extends well beyond that determinate space in all directions, to an indefinite distance. For it is much sounder, and we are much better able, to prescribe limits to the action of our thought than to the works of God.

Now, since we are taking the liberty of fashioning this matter according to our fancy, let us attribute to it, if you please, a nature in which there is nothing at all anyone cannot know as perfectly as possible. To that end, let us expressly suppose there is no form of earth, fire, or air, nor any other more particular form, such as the form of wood, stone, or metal. Nor does this matter have the qualities of being hot or cold, dry or wet, light or heavy, or having some taste, odor, sound, color, light, or similar quality in the nature of which it might be said there is something not known manifestly by everyone.

On the other hand, let us not think that this matter is the prime matter of the philosophers, which has been so well stripped of all forms and qualities that nothing remains in it that can be clearly understood. But let us conceive it as a genuine, perfectly solid body, that equally fills all the length, depth, and breadth of this great space in the midst of which we stopped our thought. Thus, each of its parts always occupies a part of this space truly proportionate to its size, such that it could not fill a larger space, nor be squeezed into a smaller, nor allow that another body might occupy its place while it remains in it.

Let us add, further, that this matter can be divided into any parts and according to any shapes we can imagine, and that each of its parts is capable of receiving in itself all the motions we can also conceive. Let us suppose, in addition, that God divides it truly into many such parts, some larger, others smaller, some of one shape, others of another, as it pleases us to fancy them. Not that God separates them from one another so that there is a void between them; let us think that the whole difference he places in them consists in the diversity of the motions he gives them. Thus, from the first instant they are created, some of them begin to move in one direction, others in another, some faster, others slower (or even, if you wish, not at all); and thereafter he makes them continue their motions according to the ordinary laws of nature. For God has so marvelously established those laws that even if we suppose he created nothing more than what I said, and even if he imposes no order or proportion on it, but composes the most confused and disordered chaos the poets could describe, they are sufficient to make the parts of that chaos disentangle themselves and dispose themselves in such good order that they will have the form of a very perfect world, one in which we would be able to see not only light, but also all the other things, both general and particular, appearing in the real world.

But before I explain this at greater length, stop again to consider this chaos a little, and note that it does not contain anything you do not know so perfectly that you could not even pretend to be ignorant of it. For, as regards the qualities I put into it, you may have noticed I assumed them to be only such as you can imagine them. And as regards the matter of which I composed the chaos, there is nothing simpler nor easier to know in inanimate creatures. The idea of that matter is so included in all the ideas our imagination can form that either you must necessarily conceive of it, or you would never imagine anything.

Nevertheless, because philosophers are so subtle, they can find difficulties in things that seem extremely clear to other people, and because the memory of their prime matter—which they know to be rather hard to conceive of—could divert them from the knowledge of which I am speaking, I must tell them at this point that, unless I am mistaken, the whole difficulty they face in their matter derives only from their wanting to distinguish it from its own quantity and from its external extension, that is, from the property it has of occupying space. In this, however, I would like them to think that they are right, for I do not intend to stop and contradict them. But they should also not find it strange that I assume the quantity of matter I described does not differ from its substance any more than number differs from things numbered. Nor should they find it strange if I conceive of its extension, or the property it has of occupying space, not as an accident, but as its true form and its essence. For they could not deny that it is very easy to conceive of in this way. And my design is not to explain things that are in fact in the real world, as they do, but only to invent, as I please, a world in which there is nothing other than what the crudest minds are capable of conceiving, and which nevertheless can be created in the same way I invented it.

If I put into this world the least obscure thing, it could happen that, within that obscurity, there might be some hidden contradiction I had not perceived, and thus without thinking, I would assume something impossible. Instead, since I can imagine distinctly everything I put into it, it is certain that even if there were nothing of this sort in the old world, God can nevertheless create it in the new world. For it is certain that he can create all the things we can imagine.

Chapter 7. The Laws of Nature of This New World[8]

But I do not want to delay any longer in telling you by what means nature by itself could untangle the confusion of the chaos I spoke of, and what are the laws God imposed on it.

You should know, first, that by nature here, I do not intend some goddess or some other sort of imaginary power. Rather, I make use of that word to signify matter itself, insofar as I consider it with all the qualities I attributed to it taken all together, under the condition that God continues to preserve it in the same fashion he created it. It follows necessarily, from the very fact that he continues to preserve it in this way, that there must be several changes in its parts which cannot, it seems to me, be properly attributed to God's action—because that action never changes—and

---

8. 1664 edition title: By What Laws and by What Means the Parts of This World Will Extricate Themselves from the Chaos and Confusion They Were In.

which I attribute to nature. And the rules by which these changes are brought about, I call the laws of nature.

To understand this better, you should recall that among the qualities of matter, we assumed that its parts had various motions from the moment they were created, and furthermore, they all touch each other from all sides without there being a void between any two of them. From this it follows necessarily that, from then on, when they began to move, they also began to change and diversify their motions by colliding with one another. And thus, if God preserves them subsequently in the same fashion he created them, he does not preserve them in the same state. That is, with God always acting the same and consequently always producing the same effect in substance there would be, as if by accident, many differences in this effect. It is easy to believe that God, who is immutable, as everyone must know, always acts in the same fashion. But without involving myself further in these metaphysical considerations, I will here set out two or three of the principal rules according to which it must be thought that God causes the nature of this new world to act, and which will suffice, I believe, to enable you to know all the others.

The first is that each specific part of matter always continues in the same state unless the collision with other bodies forces it to change that state. That is, if it has some size, it will never become smaller unless other bodies divide it. If it is round or square, it will never change that shape unless other bodies constrain it. If it is stopped in some place, it will never leave that place unless other bodies drive it out. And once it has begun to move, it will always continue to move with the same force until other bodies stop or retard it.

There is no one who does not believe that this same rule is observed in the old world with respect to size, shape, rest, and a thousand similar things. But the philosophers exempted motion from it, and yet it is the thing I desire most expressly to include in it. But do not think I intend to contradict them in this; the motion they speak of is so different from the one I conceive of, that it can easily happen that what is true of the one is not true of the other.

They themselves admit that the nature of their motion is very little understood. To render it intelligible in some way, they were not yet able to explain it more clearly than in these terms, *Motus est actus entis in potentia, prout in potentia est*, which for me are so obscure that I am compelled to leave them here in their language, because I would not know how to interpret them. (And, in fact, the words "motion is the act of a being in potency, insofar as it is in potency," are not any clearer in translation.) On the contrary, the nature of the motion I intend to speak of here is so easy to know that the geometers themselves, who among all people are the most careful to conceive very distinctly the things they consider, judged it simpler and more intelligible than the nature of their surfaces and lines, as it seems in that they explained the line by the motion of a point and the surface by the motion of a line.

The philosophers also suppose many motions they think can be accomplished without any body changing place, as those they call *motus ad formam, motus ad calorem, motus ad quantitatem* (motion with respect to form, motion with respect to heat, motion with respect to quantity), and a thousand others. As for me, I do not know of any motion other than the one which is easier to conceive of than the geometers' lines, the motion that makes bodies pass from one place to another and occupy successively all the spaces in between.

In addition, the philosophers attribute to the least of these motions a being more solid and real than they attribute to rest, which they say is nothing other than the privation of motion. As for me, I also conceive of rest as a quality, one that must be attributed to matter while it remains in one place, just as motion is a quality attributed to it while it is changing place.

Finally, the motion of which they speak has a nature so strange that, instead of all things having as an end their perfection, and striving only to preserve themselves, it has no other end nor any other aim than rest. And contrary to all laws of nature, it strives on its own to destroy itself. By contrast, the motion I suppose follows the same laws of nature as do generally all the dispositions and all the qualities found in matter, including those the scholars call *modos et entia rationis cum fundamento in re* (modes and beings of reason with foundation in things), such as *qualitates reales* (their real qualities), though I frankly confess I can find no more reality in these than in their other beings.

I suppose as a second rule that when a body pushes another, it cannot give the other any motion unless it loses as much of its own motion at the same time, nor can it take any of the other body's motion away unless its own motion is increased by as much. This rule, together with the preceding, agrees very well with all the observations in which we see one body begin or cease to move because it is pushed or stopped by another.

For, having assumed the preceding rule, we are free from the difficulty the scholars find themselves in when they want to explain why a stone continues to move for some time after leaving the hand of the person who threw it. We should ask instead: Why does the stone not always continue to move? Yet the reason is easy to give: For who can deny that the air in which the stone moves offers some resistance to it? We hear the stone whistle when it divides the air. And if we move the air with a fan or some other very light and extended body, we will even be able to feel by the weight of our hand that the air impedes motion, instead of continuing it, as some wanted to say. But if we fail to explain the effect of its resistance according to our second rule and think that the more a body can resist, the more it is capable of stopping the motion of others (as perhaps we could be persuaded at first), we will have once again great difficulty in explaining why the motion of this stone is weakened more in colliding with a soft body, whose resistance is mild, than it is when it is colliding with a harder one, which resists it more; we will also have difficulty in explaining why, as soon as it made a small effort against the latter, it immediately turns around rather than stopping or interrupting the motion it has. Instead, supposing this rule, there is no difficulty at all in this. For it teaches us that the motion of a body is not retarded by the collision with another in proportion to how much the latter resists it, but only in proportion to how much the latter's resistance is overcome, and that by obeying the law, it receives into itself the force to move which the former surrenders.

Now, although in most of the motions we see in the real world, we cannot perceive that the bodies beginning or ceasing to move are pushed or stopped by some others, this does not provide us any occasion to judge that these two rules are not being observed exactly. For it is certain that these bodies can often receive their agitation from the two elements of air and fire, which are always found among them without being perceptible, as was just said, or even from the coarser air which also cannot be perceived. And they can transfer this agitation, sometimes to that coarser air, and sometimes to the whole mass of the earth; and when it is dispersed there, it also cannot be perceived.

Even if everything our senses ever observed in the real world seemed manifestly contrary to what is contained in these two rules, the reason which taught them to me seems to be so strong that I cannot help believing myself to be required to posit them in the new world I am describing to you. For what firmer and more solid foundation could you find to establish a truth, even if you wanted to choose it at will, than the very firmness and immutability which is in God?

Now it is the case that these two rules follow manifestly from the mere fact that God is immutable and that, always acting in the same way, he always produces the same effect. For, supposing he put a certain quantity of motion in all matter in general from the first instant he created it, we must either admit that he preserves it there always or not believe that he always acts in the same way. And, assuming in addition that, from this first instant, the various parts of matter in which these motions are unequally dispersed began to retain them or to transfer them from one another according to their power to do so, then we must necessarily think that God always makes them continue in the same way. And this is what these two rules contain.

I will add as a third rule that, when a body is moving, even if its motion most often takes place along a curved line and can never take place along any line not in some way circular, as was said before, nevertheless each of its parts individually tends always to continue its motion along a straight line. And thus, their action, that is, the inclination they have to move, is different from their motion.

For example, if a wheel is made to turn on its axle, even though all its parts go in a circle—because, being joined to one another, they cannot do otherwise—nevertheless their inclination is to continue in a straight line, as it appears clearly if by chance one of them is detached from the others. For, as soon as it is free, its motion ceases to be circular and continues in a straight line.

Similarly, when a stone is whirled in a sling, not only does it go straight out as soon as it leaves the sling, but in addition, throughout the time it is in the sling, it presses against the middle of the sling and thus causes the cord to stretch. This clearly shows that it always has an inclination to go in a straight line and that it goes in a circle only under constraint.

This rule rests on the same foundation as the other two and depends only on God's preserving each thing by a continuous action, and consequently on his preserving it, not as it may have been some time earlier, but precisely as it is at the same instant he preserves it. Now, it is the case that, of all motions, only straight line motion is entirely simple: its whole nature is understood in an instant. For, to conceive of it, it suffices to think that a body is in the act of moving in a certain direction, which is the case in each instant that can be determined during the time it moves. On the other hand, to conceive of circular motion, or of any other possible motion, we must consider at least two of its instants, or rather two of its parts, and the relation between them.

But so that the philosophers, or rather the sophists, do not take the occasion here to exercise their superfluous subtleties, note that I am not saying that rectilinear motion can take place in an instant, but only that everything required to produce this motion which can be determined while they are moving is found in the bodies in each instant, and not everything required to produce circular motion.

As for example, if a stone is moving in a sling along the circle marked AB, and you consider it precisely as it is the instant it arrives at point A, you will find that it is in the act of moving, for it does not stop there, and moving in a certain direction, namely toward C, for its action is directed there at this instant.

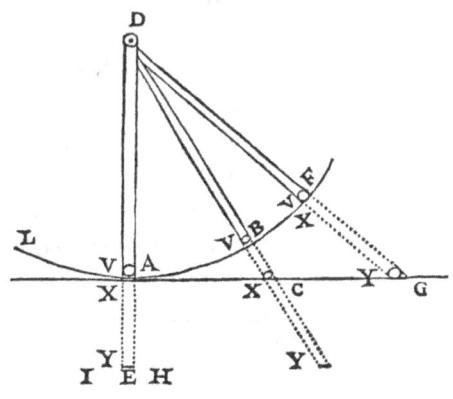

Fig. 1

But you can find nothing there which makes its motion circular. Thus, supposing that the stone now begins to leave the sling and God continues to preserve it as it is at that moment, it is certain that he will not preserve it with the inclination to go circularly along line AB, but with the inclination to go straight ahead toward point C.

According to this rule, then, we must say that God alone is the author of all the motions in the world, insofar as they exist and are straight-line motions, but that the various dispositions of matter are what render the motions irregular and curved. The theologians likewise teach us that God is also the author of all our actions, insofar as they exist and have some goodness, but the various dispositions of our wills are what can render those actions evil.

I could set out here many additional rules for determining in detail when and by how much the motion of each body can be diverted and increased or decreased by colliding with others, rules summarizing all the effects of nature. But I will be content with showing you that, apart from the three laws I explained, I wish to suppose no other but those following infallibly from the eternal truths on which mathematicians are accustomed to support their most certain and most evident demonstrations—truths, I say, according to which God himself taught us he disposed all things in number, weight, and measure. The knowledge of those laws is so natural to our souls that we cannot but judge them infallible when we conceive of them distinctly, nor can we doubt that, if God had created many worlds, the laws would be true in all of them as in this one. Thus, those who can examine sufficiently the consequences of these truths and of our rules will be able to know effects by their causes; to explain myself in the terms of the Schools, they will be able to have *a priori* demonstrations of everything that can be produced in this new world.

In order that no exception may prevent this, we will, if you please, suppose in addition that God will never produce any miracle in the new world, and intelligences or rational souls, which we will later be able to suppose in this world, will in no way disturb the ordinary course of nature.

Nonetheless, because of this, I do not promise to set out here exact demonstrations of all the things I will say. It will be enough that I will open for you the path by which you will be able to find them yourself if you take the trouble to look for them. Most minds lose interest when things are made too easy for them. And to present a picture that pleases you, I must use shadow as well as bright colors. Thus, I will be content to pursue the description I began, as if I had no other design than to tell you a fable.

Chapter 8. The Formation of the Sun and Stars of This New World[9]

Whatever inequality and confusion we might suppose God put in the beginning among the parts of matter, according to the laws he imposed on nature, it must be the case that afterward almost all of them should have been reduced to one size and moderate motion, and thus, that they took the form of the second element, as I explained before. For to consider this matter in the state it could have been before God began to move it, we must imagine it as the hardest and most solid body in the world. And since we could not push any part of such a body without also pushing or

---

9. 1664 edition title: How, in the Previously Described World, the Sun and Stars Are Formed.

pulling, by the same means, all the other parts, so we must think that the action or force of moving and dividing, first placed in some of its parts, spread out and distributed itself in all the others at the same instant, as equally as it could.

It is true that this equality could not be completely perfect. First, because there is no void at all in this new world, it was impossible for all the parts of matter to move in a straight line; but being just about equal and as easily divertible from one another, they all had to unite into some circular motions. And yet, because we suppose that God first moved them in various ways, we should not think that they all came together to turn around a single center, but around many different ones, which we can imagine to be variously situated with respect to one another.

As a result, we can conclude that they had to be naturally less agitated, or smaller, or both one and the other, at the places nearest these centers, than at those farthest away. For, all of them being inclined to continue their motion in a straight line, it is certain that the strongest, that is, the largest among those equally agitated, and the most agitated among those equally large, had to describe the largest circles, those circles most approaching a straight line. As for the matter contained within three or more of these circles, it could initially be found much less divided and less agitated than all the other matter. Further, especially since we suppose that God placed at the beginning every kind of inequality among the parts of this matter, we must think that there were then all sorts of sizes and shapes, and dispositions to move or not to move, in all ways and in all directions.

But that does not prevent them afterward from being rendered almost all fairly equal, mainly those remaining at an equal distance from the centers around which they were turning. For, not being able to move one without the others moving, the more agitated had to communicate some of their motion to those less so, and that the larger had to break and divide, to be able to pass through the same places as those preceding them, or to rise higher. And thus, in a short time all the parts were arranged in order, so that each was more or less distant from the center around which it took its course, according to whether it was more or less large and agitated, compared to others. Indeed, to the extent that size always resists speed of motion, we must think that the parts more distant from each center were those which, being a bit smaller than the ones nearer the center, were thereby much more agitated.

The same holds for their shapes, for even if we were to suppose that there were at the beginning all sorts of shapes, and that they had for the most part many angles and many sides, like the pieces exploding from a stone when it is broken, it is certain that afterward, by moving and bumping against one another, they gradually had to break off the small points of their angles, and blunt the squares of their sides, until they had almost all been made round, just as grains of sand and pebbles do when they roll with the water of a river. Thus, there cannot now be any notable difference among those parts sufficiently close, nor indeed even among those quite distant, except that they can move a bit more quickly, and be a bit smaller or larger than one another; and this does not prevent our being able to attribute the same form to all of them.

However, we must except a few, which having initially been much larger than the others, could not so easily be divided, or having had very irregular and impeding shapes, instead joined together, rather than breaking up and rounding off. Thus, they retained the form of the third element and served to make up the planets and the comets, as I will tell you later.

In addition, we need to note that the matter which came out from around the parts of the second element, to the extent that they broke and blunted the small points of their angles to become rounded, necessarily had to acquire a much faster motion than theirs, and along with it a facility for dividing and changing shape at every moment, to adapt itself to the places where it was. And so, it took the form of the first element.

I say it had to have acquired a much faster motion than theirs; and the reason is evident. For, having to go off to the side, through very narrow passages, and out of the small spaces between the parts, as they proceeded to collide head-on with one another, it had much more of a path than they to traverse in the given time.

We also need to note that what parts remain of this first element—beyond what is needed to fill the small intervals the parts of the second element, which are round, and necessarily leave around them—must draw back toward the centers around which they turn, because the parts of the second element occupy all the other more distant places. There the remaining element must compose perfectly liquid and subtle round bodies which, constantly turning much faster, and in the same direction than the parts of the second element surrounding them, have the force to increase the agitation of those parts to which they are the closest, and even of pushing them all on all sides, as they move from the center toward the circumference, just as they push one another. This takes place by an action I must soon have to explain as exactly as I can. For I warn you here in advance, we will take this action as light, as also we will take one of these round bodies, composed purely of the matter of the first element, to be the sun, and the others to be the fixed stars of the new world I am describing to you; and we will take the matter of the second element turning around them to be the heavens.

Imagine, for example, that points S, E, ε, and A are the centers of which I speak, and all matter included in space F G G F is a heaven turning around the sun marked S, all the matter of space H G G H is another such heaven turning around the star marked ε, and so on for the others. Thus, there are as many different heavens as there are stars, and since their number is indefinite, so too is that of the heavens. And the firmament is nothing other than a surface without thickness, separating all these heavens from one another.

Consider also that the parts of the second element about F, or G, are more agitated than those about K, or L, so that their speed decreases little by little, from the outside circumference of each heaven to a certain place (such as for example, to sphere K K around the sun, up to sphere L L around star ε), and then increases little by little from there to the centers of these heavens, because of the agitation of the stars found there. Thus, while the parts of the second element about K have the opportunity to describe a complete circle there around the sun, those about T, which I suppose to be ten times closer, not only have the opportunity to describe ten circles, which they would do if they moved equally fast, but perhaps more than thirty circles. Again, those parts about F, or G, which I suppose to be two or three thousand times more distant, can perhaps describe more than sixty circles. From this you will quickly understand that the highest planets must move more slowly than the lowest, that is, those closest to the sun, and all of them more slowly than comets, which are, however, more distant.

As for the size of each of the parts of the second element, we can think that it is equal among all those between the outer circumference F G G F of the heaven, up to circle K K, or even that the highest among them are a bit smaller than the lowest, provided we do not suppose the difference of their sizes to be proportionately greater than that of their speeds. But we must think, on the contrary, that, from circle K to the sun, the lowest parts are the smallest, and the difference in their sizes is even proportionately

28   *The World or Treatise on Light*

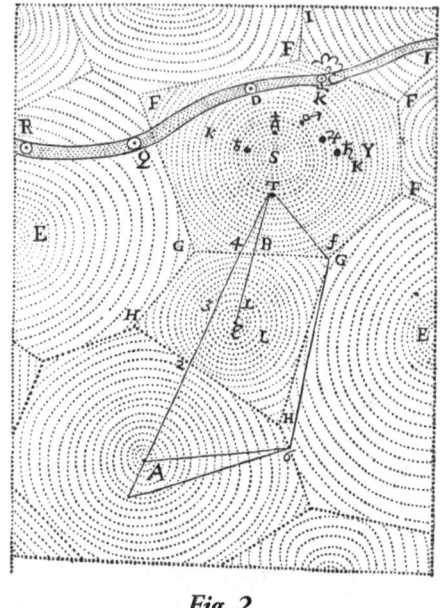

Fig. 2

greater than, or at least as proportionately as great as that of their speeds. For otherwise, since those lower parts are the strongest, because of their agitation, they would occupy the place of the highest.

Finally note that, given the way I said that the sun and the other fixed stars were formed, their bodies can be so small in relation to the heavens containing them, that even all the circles KK, LL, etc., which mark the point up to where the agitation of those bodies advances the course of the matter of the second element, will be considerable, in comparison with these heavens, only as points that mark their center. In the same way, the new astronomers consider the whole sphere of Saturn almost as a mere point in comparison to the firmament.

Chapter 9. The Origin and Course of the Planets and Comets in General, and Comets in Particular[10]

In order to begin telling you about planets and comets, consider that, given the diversity of the parts of matter I supposed, even though most of them took the form of the first or the second element by shattering and dividing when colliding with one another, this still allows two sorts to be found, which had to retain the form of the third element, namely, those whose shapes were so extended and obstructive that when they collided with one another, it was easier for several to join together, and by this means becoming larger instead of breaking up and becoming smaller; and those which, from the beginning, were the largest and most massive of all

---

10. 1664 edition title: The Origin, Course, and Other Properties of Comets, of the Planets in General and Comets in Particular.

and could well have broken up and shattered others when striking them, but not in turn being broken and shattered by them.

Now, whether you imagine that these two sorts of parts were at first very agitated, or even very little agitated, or not at all, it is certain that, afterward, they had to move with the same agitation as the matter of the heaven containing them. For if at first they were moving faster than this matter, not having been able to avoid pushing it by colliding with it in their path, they must in a short time have transferred some of their agitation to it; and if, on the contrary, they had in themselves no inclination to move, nevertheless, being surrounded on all sides by this matter of the heaven, they necessarily had to follow its course, just as we see every day boats, and other diverse bodies floating on water, both the largest and the most massive as well as the lesser ones, follow the course of the water where they are, when there is nothing else to prevent them from doing so.

And note that among the diverse bodies thus floating on water, those quite hard and massive—as boats usually are, mainly the largest and the most heavily laden—always have much more force than the water to continue their motion, even though they received their motion only from it. By contrast, very light floating bodies, such as those masses of white foam we see floating along the shores in times of storm, have less force. So, if you imagine two rivers joining one another at some place, and separating again shortly thereafter, before their waters—which must be assumed to be very calm and of sufficient equal force, but also very fast—have the occasion to mix, boats or other rather massive and heavy bodies carried by the course of the one river can easily pass into the other river, while the lighter bodies will swerve away from it, and be thrown back by the force of the water toward the places where it is the least rapid.

For example, if A B F and C D G are the two rivers, which, coming from two different directions, meet at E, then turn away from there, A B toward F and C D toward G, it is certain that boat H, following the course of river A B, must pass through E toward G, and reciprocally boat I toward F, unless they both meet at the intersection at the same time, in which case the larger and stronger will break the other. By contrast foam, tree leaves, feathers, debris, and other such light bodies that can be floating toward A, must be pushed by the course of the water containing them, not toward E and G, but toward B, where we must think that the water is less strong and less rapid than at E, since it takes its course toward B along a line approximating less a straight line.

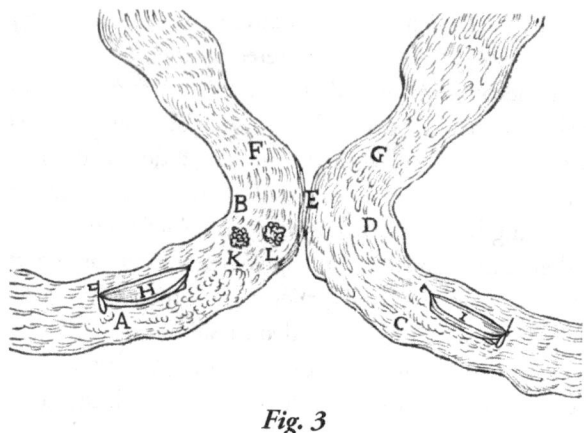

Fig. 3

Moreover, we must consider that not only these light bodies, but also others, heavier and more massive, can join upon meeting, and that, turning with the water carrying them along, several together can compose large balls, such as you see K and L, of which some, such as L, go toward E and others, such as K, go toward B, depending on whether each is more or less solid and composed of more or less large and massive parts.

Following this example, it is easy to understand that, wherever the parts of the matter that could not take the form of the second or first element were initially, all the larger and more massive among them must have shortly taken their course toward the outer circumference of the heavens containing them, and afterward passed continuously from one of these heavens into another, without ever remaining a long time in the same heaven. By contrast, all the less massive had to be pushed, each toward the center of the heaven containing them, by the course of the matter of this heaven. And, given the shapes I attributed to them, by colliding with one another, they had to join together and compose large balls which, turning in the heavens, have a motion there tempered by all the motions their parts could have, had they been separate. Thus, some go toward the circumferences of these heavens and others toward their centers.

Know that those thus tending to arrange themselves toward the center of any heaven, we should take to be the planets, and those passing across various heavens, we should take to be comets.

Now first, regarding these comets, it should be noted that there must be few of them in this new world, compared to the number of heavens.

The World or Treatise on Light

For even if there were many initially, over the course of time, in passing across various heavens, almost all of them would have collided with one another and broken each other up—just as I said the two boats do when they meet—so that now only the largest could remain.

It should also be noted that, when they pass in this way from one heaven to another, they always push before them some small amount of the matter from the heaven they are leaving, and remain enveloped by it for some time, until they have entered far enough within the limits of the other heaven. Once there, they finally rid themselves of it as if all at once, without perhaps taking more time to do so than the sun in rising in the morning on our horizon. In this way, they move much more slowly when they thus tend to leave a heaven than they do shortly after having entered it.

As you can see here, the comet taking its course along line C D Q R, having already entered rather far within the limits of heaven F G, nevertheless when it is at point C, it remains enveloped in the matter of heaven F I from which it comes, and cannot be entirely freed from it, until it is around point D. But as soon as it arrives there, it begins to follow the course of heaven F G, and thus to move a lot faster than it did before. Then, continuing its course from there toward R, its motion must again slow down little by little as it approaches point Q, both because of the resistance of heaven F G H, within the limits of which it is beginning to enter, and because, since there is less distance between S and D than between S and Q, all the matter of the heaven between S and D, where the distance is smaller, moves faster there, just as we see that rivers always flow more swiftly in the places where their bed is narrower and more confined, than in those where it is wider and more extended.

In addition, we must note that this comet should be visible to those who live at the center of heaven F G only during the time it takes to pass from D to Q, as you will soon understand more clearly when I tell you what light is. And by the same means you will know that its motion must appear to them much faster, and its body much larger, and its light much brighter at the beginning when they see it, than toward the end.

Moreover, if you consider with some care how the light coming from the comet must be spread out and distributed in all directions in the heaven, you will also be able to understand that, being very large, as we must suppose it to be, there can appear around it certain rays that sometimes extend on all sides in the form of a hazy luminescence, and sometimes collect themselves in the form of a tail on one side only, depending on the different places from which it is viewed. Thus, this comet lacks none of the particularities observed thus far in the comets we saw in the real world, at least those that should be held as true. For, if some historians, to provide a miracle warning against the Turkish crescent, tell us that in the year 1450, the moon was eclipsed by a comet passing below it, or something similar, and if the astronomers, wrongly calculating the amount of refraction from the heavens, which they do not know, and the speed of motion of comets, which is uncertain, attribute to them enough parallax to place them among the planets, or even below them, where some want to pull them as if by force, we are not obliged to believe them.

Chapter 10. Planets in General, and the Earth and Moon in Particular[11]

There are, in the same way, several things to note regarding the planets. First, even though they all tend toward the centers of the heavens containing them, this is not to say that they could ever reach those centers. For, as I already said earlier, the sun and the other fixed stars occupy them. But so that I can have you understand distinctly in which places they must stop, look, for example, at the one marked ♄,[12] which I suppose to follow the course of the matter of the heavens toward circle K; and consider that, if this planet had the slightest more force to continue its motion in a straight line than the parts of the second element surrounding it, instead of always following this circle K, it would go toward Y, and thus it would move farther away than it is from center S. Then, to the extent the parts of the second element that would surround it at Y move more quickly, and even are a bit smaller, or at least not larger than those at K, they would give it still more force to go beyond, toward F, so that it would go out to the circumference of this heaven without being able to stop anywhere in-between. Then, from there, it would easily pass into another heaven, and thus, instead of being a planet, it would become a comet.

From this you see that no star can stop anywhere in all this vast space from circle K up to the circumference of heaven FGGF, through which

---

11. 1664 edition title: The Explanation of the Planets, Mainly the Earth and Moon.

12. One of the traditional symbols for the planets which are: Mercury ☿, Venus ♀, Mars ♂, Jupiter ♃, and Saturn ♄, plus the earth, T, and the moon ☾.

comets take their course. Moreover, the planets of necessity cannot have any more force to continue their motion in a straight line than do the parts of the second element at K, when they move with the same agitation along with them; and all bodies with more force are comets.

Let us therefore think now that this planet ♄ has less force than the parts of the second element surrounding it, so that those parts following it, which are placed a little lower than it, can divert it, and instead of following circle K, make it descend toward the planet marked ♃. Planet ♄ being there, it can happen that it will be exactly as strong as the parts of the second element that will then surround it. The reason is that these parts of the second element being more agitated than those at K, they will also agitate the planet more, and being smaller as well, they will not be able to resist it as much. In this case, the planet will remain precisely balanced in the middle of them and take its course in the same direction as they do around the sun, without the planet varying in distance from it from one time to another, except insofar as they can also vary in distance from it.

But if this planet ♄, being at ♃, has even less force to continue its motion in a straight line than the matter of the heavens found there, it will be pushed still lower by the matter toward the planet marked ♂, and so on, until finally it is surrounded by a matter with neither more nor less force than it.

Thus, you see that there can be different planets, some more and others less distant from the sun, such as here ♄, ♃, ♂, T, ♀, ☿. Of these the lowest and less massive can reach the sun's surface, but the highest never pass beyond circle K which, although very large in comparison to each specific planet, is nevertheless so extremely small in comparison to the whole heaven FGGF that, as I already said before, it can be considered as its center.

But if I still did not make you understand well enough the cause for how the parts of the heaven beyond circle K, being incomparably smaller than the planets, still have more force than they to continue their motion in a straight line, consider that this force does not depend only on the amount of matter in each body, but also on the extent of its surface. For, even though when two bodies move equally fast, it is right to say that if one contains twice as much matter as the other, it also has twice the agitation, this is not to say that it has twice as much force to continue moving in a straight line; but rather it will have exactly twice as much if, in addition, its surface is exactly twice as extended, because it will always encounter twice as many other bodies resisting it, and it will have much less force, if its surface is extended much more than twice.

Now you know that the parts of the heavens are almost completely round, and thus, of all the shapes, they have the one that includes the most matter within the least surface, whereas the planets, being composed of small parts with very irregular and extended shapes, have large surfaces in proportion to the quantity of their matter. Thus, the planets can have a greater proportion of surface to quantity of matter than most of these parts of the heavens; and yet also have a smaller proportion than some of the smaller parts closest to the centers. For it must be known that between two wholly massive balls, such as these parts of the heavens, the smaller always has more surface in proportion to its quantity than the larger.

We can easily confirm all this by experience. For, pushing a large ball composed of many tree branches confusedly joined and piled on top of one another, as we must imagine are the parts of matter making up the planets, it is certain that, even if pushed by a force entirely proportional to its size, it will not be able to continue its motion as far as would another much smaller but wholly massive ball made of the same wood. On the other hand, it is also certain that we could make another ball of the same wood and wholly massive, but so extremely small that it would have much less force to continue its motion than the first. Finally, it is certain that this first ball can have more or less force to continue its motion, according to the extent that the branches composing it are more or less large and compressed.

Hence you see how various planets can be suspended within circle K at various distances from the sun, and how it is not just those outwardly appearing the largest, but those internally the most solid and the most massive that should be the most distant.

After this, we must note that, just as we observe boats following the course of a river never move as fast as the water carrying them, nor even the largest among them as fast as the smaller, so too, even though the planets follow the course of the matter of the heavens without resistance and move with the same agitation with it, this is not thereby to say that they ever move entirely as fast as that matter. Indeed, the inequality of their motion must have some relation to the inequality between the size of their mass and the smallness of the parts of the heavens surrounding them. This is because, generally speaking, the bigger a body, the easier it is for it to communicate part of its motion to other bodies, and the more difficult it is for other bodies to communicate something of their motion to it. For even though many small bodies, all acting together upon a larger one, can have as much force as it, nevertheless they can never make it move as fast in all directions as they do, because, if they agree in some of the motions they communicate to it, at the same time they infallibly differ in other motions they cannot communicate to it.

Now two things follow from this, which seem to me very significant. The first is that the matter of the heavens must not only make the planets turn around the sun, but also around their own center (except when there is some specific cause preventing them from doing so); further, the matter must compose, around the planets, small heavens that move in the same direction as the greater one. The second is that, if there are two planets unequal in size but disposed to take their course in the heaven at the same distance from the sun, if one of them is exactly as massive as the other is larger, then the smaller of the two, having a faster motion than the larger one, must become joined to the small heavens around the larger planet and turn continually with it.

For since the parts of the heavens at A, for example, move faster than the planet marked T, which they push toward Z, it is evident that they must be diverted by it and constrained to take their course toward B. I say toward B rather than toward D. For, having inclination to continue their motion in a straight line, they must go toward the outside of circle ACZN, which they describe, rather than toward center S. Now, passing thus from A to B, they force planet T to turn with them about its center; reciprocally this planet, by so turning, gives them occasion to take their course from B to C, then to D, and to A, and thus to form around it a particular heaven, with which it must afterward continue to move from the direction called west, toward the one called east, not only around the sun, but also around its own center.

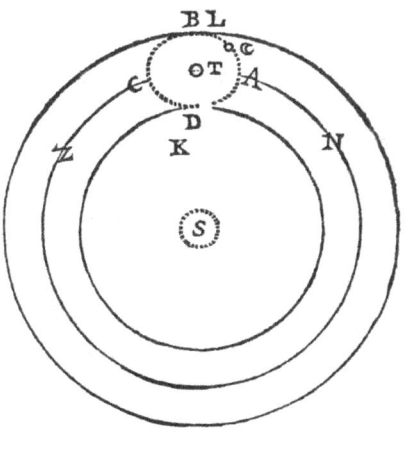

Fig. 4

Moreover, knowing that the marked planet ☾ is disposed to take its course along circle NACZ, just as the planet marked T, and that it must move faster because it is smaller, it is easy to understand that, wherever it may have been in the heavens at the beginning, in a short time it had to tend toward the exterior surface of small heaven ABCD and, once having joined it, it must thereafter follow its course around T along with the parts of the second element at this surface.

For, since we suppose it would have just as much force as the matter of this heavens to turn along circle NACZ if the other planet were not there, then we must consider that it has a bit more force to turn along circle ABCD, because it is smaller and consequently it always moves as far away as possible from center T. In the same way, a stone, moving in a sling always tends away from the center of the circle it is describing. This planet, however, being at A, will not thereby deviate toward L, since it would then enter a location in the heaven whose matter had the force to push it back toward circle NACZ. And in the same way, being at C, it will not go down toward K, especially since it would be surrounded by a matter that would provide it with the force to go up toward this same circle NACZ. It will not descend from B to Z, much less from D toward N, since it could not go as easily or as fast as it could toward C and toward A. Thus, it must remain as if attached to the surface of the small heaven ABCD and turn continuously with it about T. This prevents it forming another small heaven around it, which would make it turn again around its center.

I do not add here how a greater number of planets can be found joined together and taking their course around one another, such as those the new astronomers observed around Jupiter and Saturn. For I did not undertake to say everything, and I spoke in particular of these two planets, only to represent to you, by the planet marked T, the earth we inhabit, and by the one marked ☾, the moon turning about it.

Chapter 11. Weight[13]

But now I want you to consider what the weight of this earth is, that is, the force uniting all its parts, which makes them all tend toward its center, each more or less, according to whether they are more or less large and solid. This force is nothing other and consists in nothing other than the

---

13. 1664 edition title: What Weight Is.

parts of the small heaven surrounding it, turning much faster than its parts around its center, also tend to move away from it with more force, and as a result to push the parts of the earth back toward its center. You may find some difficulty in this, given what I said earlier that the most massive and most solid bodies, such as I supposed those of the comets to be, tended to move toward the circumferences of the heavens, and only those less massive and solid were driven back to their centers, for from this it should follow that only the less solid parts of the earth could be pushed toward its center and the others should move away from it. But note that, when I said that the most solid and most massive bodies tended to move away from the center of some heaven, I supposed that they were already moving with the same agitation as the matter of that heaven. For it is certain that, if they did not yet begin to move, or if they are moving less fast than required to follow the course of this matter, they must at first be driven by it toward the center around which it turns; indeed, it is certain that, to the extent they are larger and more solid, they will be pushed with more force and speed. And yet if they are massive enough to compose comets, this does not hinder them from tending soon afterward toward the exterior circumferences of the heavens; the agitation they acquired in descending toward one of their centers will infallibly give them the force to go beyond and ascend toward its circumference.

To understand this more clearly, consider earth EFGH, with water 1.2.3.4, and air 5.6.7.8, which, as I will tell you later, are only composed of some of the less solid of its parts and make up a single mass with it. Next also consider the matter of the heaven, which fills not only all the space between circles ABCD and 5.6.7.8, but also all the small intervals below it among the parts of the air, water, and earth. Consider that, since this heaven and this earth are turning together around center T, all their parts tend to move away from it, but those of the

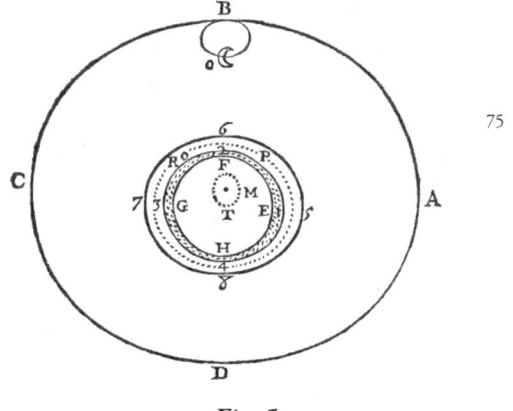

Fig. 5

heaven much more than those of the earth, because they are much more agitated. Indeed, among the parts of the earth, the most agitated in the same direction as those of the heaven tend to move more away from the center than the others. Thus, if all the space beyond circle ABCD were void, that is, were filled only with a matter that could not resist the actions of other bodies nor produce any considerable effect (for this is how we must construe the name void), all the parts of the heaven in circle ABCD would leave it first, then those of the air and the water would follow, and finally also those of the earth, each all the more quickly to the extent it finds itself less attached to the rest of the mass. In the same way, a stone leaves the sling in which it is being moved as soon as the cord is released, and dust one throws on a top while it is turning immediately flies away from it in all directions.

Then consider that, since there is no void space beyond circle ABCD where the parts of the heaven contained within this circle can go, unless at the same instant others completely like them enter their place, the parts of earth also cannot move away any farther than they do from center T, unless as many parts of the heaven or other terrestrial parts descend in their place as are needed to fill it. Nor, conversely, can they move closer to it unless just as many other parts rise in their place. Thus, they are all opposed to one another, each one being opposed to those that must enter their place, in case they rise, and in the same way, to those that must enter in case they descend, just as the two sides of a balance are opposed to one another. That is, just as one side of the scale cannot be raised or lowered unless the other at the same time does the opposite, and the heavier one always wins over the other, so also stone R, for example, is so opposed to the quantity (exactly the same size) of air above it whose place it would have to occupy in case it moved away farther from center T, that this air would necessarily have to descend to the extent the stone rose. And in the same way it is so opposed to another such quantity of air below it whose place it must occupy in case it moved closer to this center, that the stone must descend when this air rises.

Now it is evident that, since this stone contains in itself much more of the matter of the earth than a quantity of air of equal extent, and in recompense contains that much less of the matter of the heaven, and since its terrestrial parts are less agitated by the matter of the heaven than the parts of this air, it should not have the force to rise above it, but the quantity of air, on the contrary, must have the force to make it descend below it. Thus, the quantity of air is light, in comparison with the stone, but heavy when it is compared with the pure matter of the heaven. In this way you see that each part of the terrestrial bodies is pressed toward T: not indifferently by all the matter surrounding it, but only by a quantity of this matter exactly equal to its size, which quantity, being below it, can take its place if the part moves down. This is why, among the parts of any single body we call homogeneous, such as those of air or water, the lowest ones are not notably more pressed than the highest, and a person, down below very deep water, does not feel it weighing on his back more heavily than if he were swimming right above it.

But if it seems to you that the matter of the heaven, in making stone R fall toward T, below the air surrounding it, should also make it go toward 6, or toward 7, that is, toward the west or toward the east, faster than this air, so that the stone does not fall in a straight plumb line, as heavy bodies do on the real earth, consider first that all the terrestrial parts contained in circle 5, 6, 7, 8 being pressed toward T by the matter of the heaven, in the way I just explained, and having in addition very irregular and diverse shapes, must join and cling to one another, and thus compose only one mass. This mass is carried wholly by the course of heaven ABCD in such a way that, while it turns, those of its parts at 6, for example, always remain face to face with those at 2 and at F, without deviating noticeably one way or the other, unless winds or other specific causes force them to do so.

And note also that this little heaven ABCD turns much faster than this earth, but those of its parts caught in the pores of the terrestrial bodies cannot turn notably faster than these bodies around center T, although they move much faster in various other directions, according to the disposition of these pores.

Next, you should know that, even though the matter of the heaven makes stone R approach this center, because it tends to move away from it with more force than the stone, still the matter cannot force the stone to go back toward the west, even though the matter also tends with more force than the stone to go toward the east. For you should consider that this matter of the heaven tends to move away from center T, because it tends to continue its motion in a straight line, but it tends to move from the west to east, only because it tends to continue its motion at the same speed, and moreover it is indifferent to whether it is at 6 or at 7.

Now it is evident that the matter moves a bit more in a straight line while making stone R fall toward T than it would in leaving it at R; but it could not move so fast toward the east, if it made it move back toward the west, as it could if it left the stone in its place or even if it pushed the stone in front of it.

However, you should also know that even though this matter of the heaven has more force to cause stone R to descend toward T than to make the air surrounding it descend there, it should not have more force to push the stone in front of it from west to east, nor consequently to cause the stone to move faster in this direction than the air. You should consider that there is just as much of this matter of the heaven acting against the stone to cause it to descend toward T and using all its force to that end, as there is terrestrial matter in the composition of the stone's body; moreover, the more terrestrial matter there is in the stone than in a quantity of air of equal extent, the more the stone must be pressed much more toward T than is this air. But to make the stone turn toward the east, all the matter of the heaven contained in circle R must act on it, as well as on all the terrestrial parts of the air contained in that same circle. Thus, since there is no more action on it than on this air, it should not turn faster than the air in that direction.

And you can understand as a result that the reasons many philosophers use to refute the motion of the true earth have no force against the motion of the earth I am describing to you. They say, for example, that if the earth moved, heavy bodies could not descend in a plumb line toward its center, but rather would move here and there toward the heaven, and cannons, pointed toward the west should carry much farther than if pointed toward the east, and we should always feel great winds in the air and hear great noises. These and similar things occur only in the event one supposes that the earth is not carried by the course of the heaven surrounding it but moved by some other force and in some other direction than that heaven.

Chapter 12. The Ebb and Flow of the Sea

After having thus explained the weight of the parts of this earth, caused by the action of the matter of the heaven in its pores, I must now speak to you about a certain motion of its whole mass, caused by the presence of the moon, as well as some peculiarities depending on it.

For this effect, consider the moon at B, for example, where you can suppose it to be motionless in comparison to the speed at which the matter of the heaven below it moves. Consider also that this matter of the heaven, having less space to pass through between O and 6 than between B and 6 (if the moon does not occupy the space between O and B), and consequently having to move a little faster there, cannot fail to have the force to push the whole earth a bit toward D, so that its center T moves away, as you see, a bit from point M, which is the center of small heaven ABCD. For nothing other than the sole course of matter in this heaven keeps the earth where it is. And because air 5, 6, 7, 8 and water 1, 2, 3, 4 surrounding this earth are liquid bodies, it is evident that the same force pressing the earth in this way must also sink them toward T, not only from side 6, 2, but also from its opposite 8, 4, and in recompense cause them to rise in places 5, 1, and 7, 3; thus, the surface EFGH of the earth remaining round, because it is hard, that of water 1, 2, 3, 4, and air 5, 6, 7, 8, which are liquid, must form an oval.

Then consider that, since the earth is in the meanwhile turning around its center, and in this way producing the days, which can be divided into 24 hours like we do ours, side F, now facing the moon and on which water 2 is for this reason less high, must in six hours be facing the place of the heaven marked C, where this water will be higher, and in 12 hours facing the place in the heaven marked D, where this water will again be lower. Thus, the sea, which is represented by water 1, 2, 3, 4, must have its ebb and flow around this earth once every six hours, just as it has around the earth we inhabit.

Consider also that, while this earth turns from E through F to G, that is, from west through the meridian to east, the swelling of the water and the air that remains at 1 and 5, and at 3 and 7, passes from its east side toward the west, causing there an ebb without flow, quite similar to the one which, according to the report of our helmsmen, makes navigation on our seas from east to west much easier than from west to east.

And so as not to forget anything at this point, let us add that each month the moon makes the same circuit as the earth does each day, thus, causing points 1, 2, 3, 4, that mark the highest and the lowest tides to advance gradually toward the east. Hence these tides do not change precisely every six hours, but lag behind by approximately a fifth part of an hour each time, as also do those of our seas.

Consider, further, that small heaven A B C D is not exactly round but extends a bit more freely at A and C and moves proportionately more slowly there than at B and at D, where it cannot so easily break the course of the matter of the other heaven containing it. Thus, the moon, which always remains as if attached to its external surface, must move a bit faster, and deviate less in its path, and consequently cause the ebb and flow of the sea to be much greater when the moon is at B, where it is full, and at D, where it is new, than when it is at A and C, where it is only half full. Peculiarities entirely like these are also observed by astronomers on the real moon, although they may not so easily explain them through the hypotheses they use.

As for the other effects of this moon, which are different when it is full than when it is new, they manifestly depend on its light. And as for the other peculiarities of ebb and flow, they depend in part on the different situation of the seacoasts, and in part on the winds prevailing at the time and place we observe them. Finally, as for the other general motions of the earth and the moon, as well as of the other stars and the heavens, either you can understand them enough from what I said, or else they are not relevant to my topic, and not falling under the same subject as those I spoke of, they would take me too long to describe. So, all that remains for me here is to explain this action of the heavens and the stars I earlier said should be taken for their light.

Chapter 13. Light[14]

I already said several times that the bodies turning in circles always tend to move away from the centers of the circles they describe; but here I must determine more specifically in what directions the parts of the matter of which the heavens and the stars are composed tend.

And to this end we must know that, when I say a body tends in some direction, I do not thereby want anyone to imagine it has in itself a thought or a volition carrying it there, but only that it is disposed to move there: whether it truly moves there, or whether some other body prevents it from doing so. I use the word "to tend" mainly in this latter sense, because it seems to signify some effort, and every effort presupposes some resistance. Now, to the extent that there are often diverse causes that, acting together

---

14. 1664 edition title: What Light Consists Of.

on the same body, impede the effect of one another, we can, according to various considerations, say that the same body tends in different directions at the same time. Thus we just said that the parts of the earth tend to move away from its center insofar as they are considered in isolation, and they tend, on the contrary, to move closer to it insofar as we consider the force of the parts of the heaven pushing them there, and further, they tend to move away from it, if we consider them as opposed to other terrestrial parts composing bodies more massive than them.

Thus, for example, the stone turning in a sling following circle AB tends toward C when it is at point A, if we solely consider its agitation; and it tends circularly from A to B, if we consider its motion as regulated and determined by the length of the cord retaining it; and finally, the same stone tends toward E, if, without considering the part of its agitation of which the effect is not impeded, we oppose the other part of it to the resistance the sling continually makes to it.

But to understand this last point distinctly, imagine the inclination this stone has to move from A to C, as if it were composed of two other inclinations, one turning around circle AB, and the other going straight up along line VXY. Imagine the inclinations in such proportion that, the stone being at the place on the circle marked V when the sling is at the place on the circle marked A, it should afterward be at the place marked X when the sling is at B, and at the place marked Y when it is at F, and thus always remain in straight line ACG. Then, knowing that one of the parts of its inclination, namely the one carrying it along circle AB, is in no way impeded by the sling, you will clearly see that the stone finds resistance only for the other part, namely for the one that would cause it to move along line DVXY, if it were not impeded. Consequently, it tends, that is, it makes an effort, only to move directly away from center D. And note that, considered thus, when the stone is at point A, it tends so truly toward E that it is not at all more disposed to move toward H than toward I, although we could easily be persuaded of the contrary, if we failed to consider the difference between the motion it already has and the inclination to move that remains with it.

Now you should think of each of the parts of the second element composing the heavens in the same way as of this stone, that is, those at E, for example, tend of their own inclination only toward P, but the resistance of the other parts of the heaven above them cause them to tend, that is, dispose them to move along circle ER. This resistance in turn, opposed to the inclination they have to continue their motion in a straight line, makes

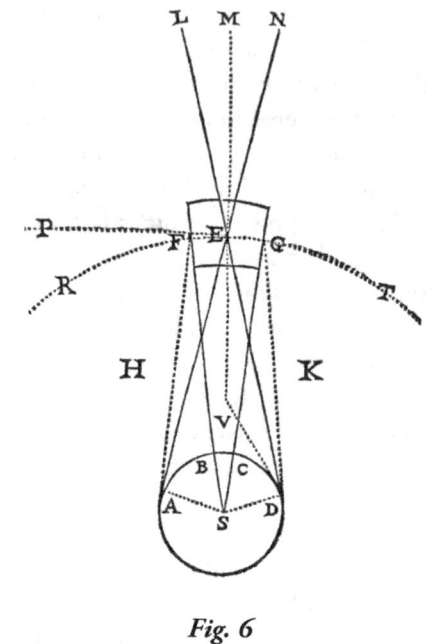

Fig. 6

them tend, that is, is the cause why they make an effort to move toward M. Thus, judging all the others in the same way, you see in what sense we can say that they tend toward the places directly opposite to the center of the heaven they compose.

But there is more to consider in the parts of the heaven than in a stone turning in a sling. The parts are continually pushed, both by all the similar parts between them and by the star occupying the center of their heaven, and even by the matter of this star, and they are not at all pushed by the others. For example, those at E are not pushed by those at M, T, R, K, or H, but only by all those between the two lines A F and D G, together with the matter of the sun. This is why they tend, not only toward M, but also toward L and N, and generally toward all the points that can be reached by the rays, or straight lines, coming from some part of the sun and passing through the place they are.

But, to make the explanation of all this easier, I want you to consider the parts of the second element on their own, and as if all the spaces occupied by the matter of the first element, both where the sun is and elsewhere, were void. Indeed, because there are no better means of knowing if a body is being pushed by some others than to see if these others actually advance toward the place where it is, to fill the place in case it was void, I also want you to imagine that the parts of the second element at E are removed from it; that being posited, I want you to note, in the first place, that none of those above the circle TER, such as at M, are at all disposed to fill their place, especially as, on the contrary, they tend to move away from it. Then also note that those in this circle, namely at T, are no more disposed to do so, for even though they really move from T toward G along the course of the whole heaven, nevertheless, because those at F also move with the same speed toward R, space E, which must be imagined to be mobile like them, would not fail to remain void between G and F, if others did not come to fill it from elsewhere. And third, those below this circle but not contained between lines AF and DG, such as those at H and K, also do not tend at all to advance toward space E to fill it, even though the inclination they have to move away from point S disposes them there in some way, just as the weight of a stone disposes it, not only to descend along a straight line into the open air, but also to roll sideways on the slope of a mountain, in case it cannot descend any other way.

Now, the reason that impedes them from tending toward this space is that all the motions continue, as far as possible, in a straight line; and consequently, when nature has several ways to achieve the same effect, it always infallibly follows the shortest. For, if the parts of the second element at K, for example, advanced toward E, all those closer to the sun than they are would also advance at the same instant toward the place they were leaving; and thus, the effect of their motion would be only that space E would be filled and there would be another space of equal magnitude in the circumference A B C D that would become void at the same time. But it is manifest that this same effect can follow much better if those parts between lines A F and D G advance straight away toward E; and consequently, when there is nothing to impede the latter, the others do not tend at all toward E, any more than a stone ever tends to descend obliquely toward the center of the earth when it can fall there in a straight line.

Finally, consider that all the parts of the second element between lines A F and D G must advance together toward space E to fill it at the instant it is void. For, even though it is only the inclination they have to move away from point S that carries them toward E, and this inclination causes those between lines B F and C G to tend more directly toward E, those remaining between lines A F, B F and D G, C G, you will nevertheless see that these latter parts do not fail to be as disposed as the others to go there, if you take note of the effect that must follow from their motion. That effect, as I just said, is simply that space E is filled and that there is another of equal size in circumference A B C D that becomes void at the same time. For the change of position occurring to them in the other places they were filling previously and that remain full of them afterward, is not at all significant, since they are supposed to be so equal and similar to one another, that it does not matter by which parts each of these places is filled. Note however, that we should not conclude from this that they are all equal, but only that the motions of which their inequality can be the cause are not relevant to the action of which we are speaking.

Now, there is no shorter way of filling one part of space E while another at D, for example, becomes void, than if all the parts of the matter on straight right line D G or D E advance together toward E. For, if there were only those between lines B F and C G that were to advance first toward this space E, they would leave another space below them at V into which those at D would have to come. In this way, the same effect that can be produced by the motion of matter in straight line D G or D E would be produced by the motion of what is in curved line D V E, which is contrary to the laws of nature.

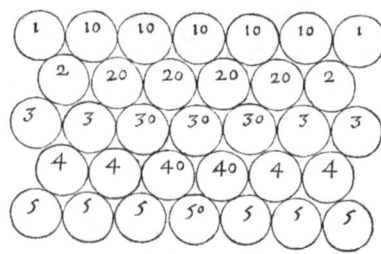

Fig. 7

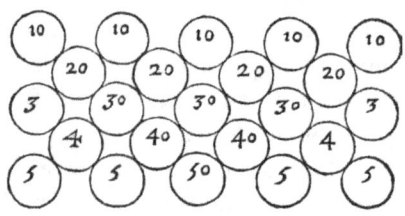

Fig. 8

But you may find here some difficulty in understanding how the parts of the second element between lines A F and D G can advance all together toward E, given that, since the distance between A and D is greater than the one between F and G, the space they must enter to advance in this way is narrower than the one from which they must leave. If so, consider that the action by which they tend to move away from the center of their heaven does not force them to touch those of their neighbors at the same distance as they are from this center, but only to touch those slightly farther from it. Thus, the weight of the small balls 1, 2, 3, 4, 5 does not force those marked with the same number to touch one another, but only forces those marked 1 or 10 to rest on those marked 2 or 20, and these to rest on those marked 3 or 30, and so on. Hence, these little balls can well be arranged not only as you see them in figure 7, but also as they are in figures 8 or 9, and in a thousand other different ways.

Next, consider that those parts of the second element, moving separately from one another, as it was said earlier that they must do, can never be arranged like the balls in figure 7. However, this is the only way in which the proposed difficulty can occur. For we could not suppose between those of its parts at the same distance from the center of their heaven an interval so small that it would not suffice to conceive that the inclination they have to move away from this center must cause those between lines AF and DG to advance all together toward space E when it is void; thus, you see in figure 9, compared with figure 10, that the weight of the small balls 40, 30, etc., must cause them to fall all together toward the space occupied by the one marked 50 as soon as the latter can leave it.

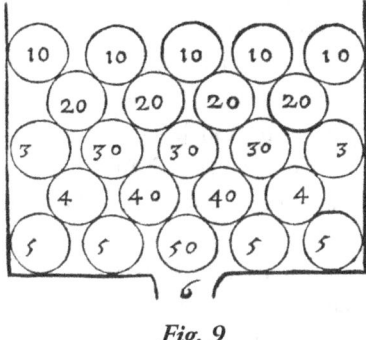

Fig. 9

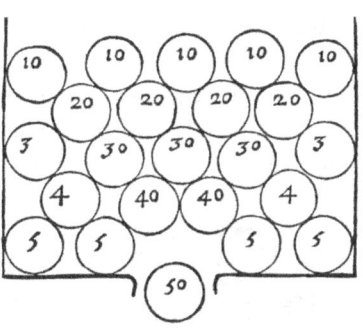

Fig. 10

And we can clearly see here how those of the balls marked with the same number are arranged in a space narrower than the one from which they leave, namely, by moving closer to one another. We can also see that the two balls marked 40 must fall a bit faster and move proportionately a bit closer to one another than the three marked 30, and these must move faster and closer than the four marked 20, and so on.

As a result of this, you will perhaps tell me that, as it appears in figure 10, the two balls 40, 40, after having fallen a small amount, however little, come to touch each other (which is why they stop without being able to fall farther). In the same way, the parts of the second element that must advance toward E will stop before having completely filled the whole space we supposed to be there.

But I reply that they cannot advance the slightest toward E without it being sufficient enough to prove perfectly what I said, namely that, since the whole space there is already filled by some body, whatever it may be, the parts continually press on that body and make an effort against it, as if to chase it out of its place.

Further, I reply that, since their other motions, which continue in them while they are advancing in this way toward E, do not allow them for a single moment to remain arranged in the same way, they prevent them from touching one another, or rather cause them immediately to separate again upon touching, and thus do not stop advancing without interruption toward space E, until it is completely filled. So, we cannot conclude from this anything else, other than the force with which they tend toward E is perhaps, as it were trembling, and increases and relaxes with various small tremors as the parts change position. And this seems to be a property well suited to light.

Now if you have understood all this sufficiently, by supposing spaces E and S and all the small angles between the parts of the heaven to be empty, you will understand it even better by supposing them to be filled with the matter of the first element. For the parts of this first element in space E cannot prevent those of the second between lines AF and DG from advancing to fill it in just the same way as they would if it were void, because being extremely subtle and extremely agitated, they are always as ready to leave the places they occupy as any other body can be to enter them. And for this same reason, those parts occupying the small angles between the parts of the heaven give way without resistance to those coming from space E and tending toward point S. I say toward S rather than toward any other place because the other bodies, being more united and larger and thus have more force, tend to move away from it.

Indeed, it should be noted that they pass from E toward S between the parts of the second element that go from S to E without impeding each other in any way. Thus, the air enclosed in hourglass XYZ rises from Z toward X through sand Y, which however, does not fail to fall toward Z.

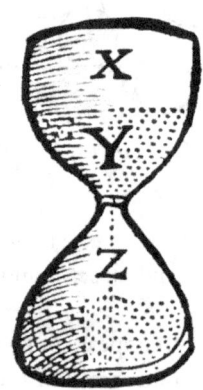

Fig. 11

Finally, the parts of this first element in space ABCD, where they compose the body of the sun, turning in a circle very rapidly around point S, tend to move away from it in all directions in a straight line, according to what I just explained. By this means, all those in line SD together push the part of the second element at point D, and all those in line SA push what is at point A, and so on. They do so in such a way that this alone suffices to cause all those parts of the second element between lines AF and DG to advance toward space E, although in themselves, they might have no inclination to do so.

Moreover, since they must thus advance toward this space E when it is occupied only by the matter of the first element, it is certain that they also tend to go there, even though it is filled by some other body and, therefore, that they push and make an effort against that body, as if to drive it out of its place. Thus, if the eye of a man were at point E, it would actually be pushed, both by the sun and by all the matter of the heaven between lines AF and DG.

Now it should be known that the people of this new world will be of such a nature that, when their eyes are pushed in this way, they will have a sensation altogether similar to the one we have of light, as I will say more fully later on.

Chapter 14. The Properties of Light

But I want to pause here a bit longer to explain the properties of the action by which their eyes can be thus pushed. For they all relate so perfectly to those we note in light that, when you have considered them, I am sure you will admit, like me, that there is no need to imagine in the stars or in the heavens any quality other than this action called by the name of light.

The principal properties of light are: 1) that it extends circularly in all directions around the bodies called luminous; 2) and to any distance; 3) and in an instant; 4) and usually in straight lines that must be taken for rays of light; 5) and several of these rays, coming from different points, can come together at the same point; 6) or, coming from the same point, can go to different points; 7) or, coming from different points, and going to different points, can pass through the same point without impeding one another; 8) and they can also sometimes impede one another, namely, when their force is very unequal and that of some rays much greater than that of the others; 9) and finally, they can be diverted by reflection; 10) or by refraction; 11) and their force can be increased; 12) or diminished by the different dispositions or qualities of the matter receiving them. These are the principal qualities we observe in light, which all agree with this action, as you will see.

1) The reason this action should extend in all directions around luminous bodies is evident, because the action proceeds from the circular motion of their parts.

2) It is also evident that it can extend to any distance. For example, supposing the parts of heaven between AF and DG are already of themselves disposed to advance toward E, as we said they are, we also cannot doubt that the force with which the sun pushes those at ABCD should also extend out to E, even though there is a greater distance from the one to the other than there is from the highest stars of the firmament to us.

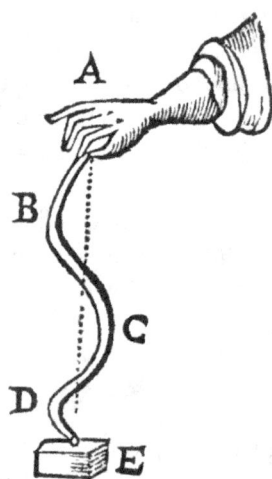

Fig. 12

3) And knowing that the parts of the second element between AF and DG all touch and press one another as much as possible, we also cannot doubt that the action by which the first ones are pushed must pass to the last in an instant, in just the same way that the force with which we push one end of a stick passes to the other end in an instant. Or rather—so that you cannot object on the basis that these parts are not attached to one another as those of a stick are—in just the same way as in figure 9, as the small ball marked 50 falls toward 6, the others marked 10 also fall toward 6 at the same instant.

4) As for the lines along which this action is communicated and which are properly light rays, it should be noted that they differ from the parts of the second element by means of which this same action is communicated, and they are not something material in the medium through which they pass but designate only in what direction and according to what determination the luminous body acts on the body it illuminates. Thus, we should not fail to conceive them as exactly straight,

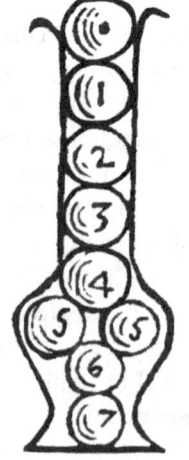

Fig. 13

even though the parts of the second element serving to transmit this action, that is, light, can hardly ever be so directly placed one on the other that they compose straight lines. In the same way, you can easily conceive that hand A pushes body E along straight-line AE even though it only pushes it through the intermediary of stick BCD, which is twisted. And in the same way also the ball marked 1 pushes the one marked 7 through the intermediary of the two marked 5 and 5, as directly as through the intermediary of the others 2, 3, 4, 6.

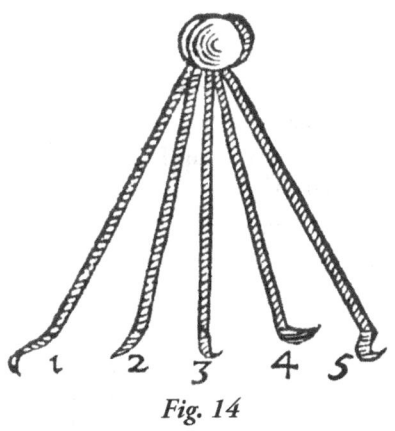

Fig. 14

5–6) You can also easily conceive how several of these rays, coming from different points, meet at the same point, or coming from the same point, go to different points, without impeding or depending on one another. As you can see in figure 6, several of them come from points ABCD and assemble at point E; and several come from the single point D and extend, one toward E, the other toward K, and thus toward an infinity of other places. In just the same way, the different forces with which cords 1, 2, 3, 4, 5 are pulled all assemble in the pulley, and the resistance of this pulley extends to all the different hands pulling these cords.

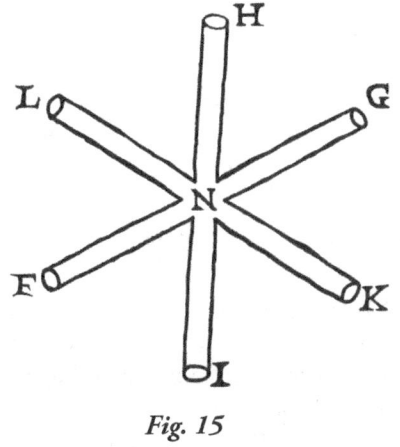

Fig. 15

7) But to conceive how several of these rays, coming from different points and going toward different points, can pass through the same point without preventing one another, just as in figure 6, two rays AN and DL pass through point E, we must consider that each of the parts of the second element is capable of receiving several different motions at the same

time. Thus, for example, the part at point E can be pushed as a whole toward L by the action coming from the place on the sun marked D and, at the same time, toward N, by what comes from the place marked A. You will understand this even better if you consider that we can push the air at the same time from F toward G, from H toward I, and from K toward L, through the three tubes FG, HI, and KL, even though these tubes are so joined at point N that all the air passing through the middle of one of them must also necessarily pass through the middle of the other two.

8) And this same comparison can be used to explain how a strong light impedes the effect of weaker lights. For, if we push the air through F much more strongly than through H or through K, it will not tend at all toward I or toward L, but only toward G.

9–10) As for reflection and refraction, I already sufficiently explained them elsewhere.[15] However, because I used the example of the motion of a ball there, instead of speaking of light rays, in order to make my account more intelligible, it still remains for me here to have you consider that the action, or inclination to move, transmitted from one place to another by means of several bodies touching one another and continually filling all the space between them follows exactly the same path along which this same action could make the first of these bodies move, if the others were not in its way. The only other difference is that it would take time for this body to move, whereas the action in it can, through the intermediary of those touching it, extend to all sorts of distances in an instant. From this it follows that, just as a ball is reflected when it strikes against the wall of a tennis court and undergoes refraction when it enters or leaves obliquely into water, likewise, when light rays encounter a body not allowing them to pass beyond it, they must be reflected, and when they enter obliquely into some place through which they can extend more or less easily than through the one from which they are coming, they must also be diverted and undergo refraction at the point of this change.

11–12) Finally, the force of the light is not only more or less great in each place according to the quantity of the rays assembling there, but it can also be increased or diminished by the different dispositions of the bodies in the places through which it passes. In the same way, the speed of a ball or a stone pushed in the air can be increased by winds blowing in the same direction it is moving and diminished by their contraries.

---

15. *Dioptrics* II, AT VI, 93–105 and 89–93.

Chapter 15. That the Face of the Heaven of This New World Must Appear to Its Inhabitants Entirely Like That of Our World[16]

Having thus explained the nature and the properties of the action I took for light, I must also explain how, by its means, the inhabitants of the planet I assumed for the earth can see the face of their heaven as wholly like that of ours.

First, there is no doubt that they must see the body marked S as completely full of light, and like our sun, since this body sends rays from all points of its surface toward their eyes. And because it is much closer to them than the stars, it must appear much greater to them. It is true that the parts of small heaven ABCD turning around the earth offer some resistance to these rays; but because all the parts of the large heaven between S and D strengthen them, those between D and T, being comparatively few in number, can only take away very little of their force from them. And even all the action of the parts of large heaven FGGF is not enough to impede the rays of many fixed stars from reaching the earth from the side not illuminated by the sun.

For it must be understood that the great heavens, that is, those with a fixed star or sun for their center, may perhaps be rather unequal in size, but must always be of exactly equal force, such that all the matter, for example, in line S B must tend as strongly toward ε as the one in line ε B tends toward S. For, if they did not have this equality among them, they would infallibly be destroyed in a short time, or at least they would change until they had acquired it.

Now since the whole force of ray S B, for example, is only precisely equal to that of ray εB, it is manifest that the force of ray T B, which is less, cannot impede the force of ray εB from extending to T. And in the same way it is evident that star A can extend its rays up to earth T, to the extent that the matter of the heaven between A and 2 helps them more than that between 4 and T resists them, and to the extent as that between 3 and 4 helps them no less than that between 3 and 2 resists them. And so, judging others proportionately, you can understand that these stars cannot appear less confusedly arranged, nor less in number, nor less unequal among one another, than those we see in the real world.

---

16. 1664 edition title: The Way the Sun and Stars Act against Our Eyes.

But you must still consider, regarding their arrangement, that they can hardly ever appear in their actual places. For example, the one marked ε appears as if it were in straight line T B, and the other marked A as if it were in straight line T 4. The reason for this is that since the heavens are unequal in size, the surfaces separating them are almost never so arranged that the rays passing through, going from these stars toward the earth, meet them at right angles. And when the rays meet them obliquely, it is certain, according to what was demonstrated in the *Dioptrics*,[17] that they must bend and undergo much refraction to the extent they pass much more easily through one side of this surface than through the other. And we must suppose these lines T B, T 4, and the like to be so extremely long in comparison with the diameter of the circle that the earth describes around the sun that, wherever the earth is on this circle, the people on it always see the stars as fixed and attached to the same places on the firmament, that is, to use the terms of the astronomers, they cannot observe parallax in the stars.

Consider also, regarding the number of these stars, that the same one can often appear in different places because of the different surfaces diverting its rays toward the earth. For example, here the one marked A appears both on line T 4 by means of ray A 2 T 4 and on line T f by means of ray A 6 f T. In the same way, the objects are multiplied when we look at them through lenses or other transparent bodies cut along several faces.

Moreover, regarding their size, consider that they must appear much smaller than they are, because of their extreme distance, and even for this reason the greater part of them cannot appear at all, and others only insofar as the rays of several joined together make the parts of the firmament through which they pass a little whiter and like certain stars astronomers call nebulous, or to that great belt of our heaven the poets pretend to be whitened by Juno's milk. However, it suffices to suppose the less distant stars to be approximately equal to our sun for us to judge that they can appear as large as the largest of our world.

Generally, all the bodies sending out stronger rays against the eyes of observers than those surrounding them also appear larger proportionately than them, and therefore, these stars must always appear larger than the parts of their heavens equal and surrounding them, as I will explain later. Further, surfaces F G, G G, G F, and ones like them, where the refractions

---

17. AT VI, 81–93.

of their rays occur, can be curved in such a way that their size is greatly increased, and they are increased even when completely flat.

Moreover, it is very likely that these surfaces, being in a very fluid matter that never ceases to move, should always shake and oscillate somewhat, and therefore, the stars we see through them should appear to scintillate, as if vibrating, just as ours do, and even, because of their vibration, appear a little larger. In this way the image of the moon appears larger at the bottom of a lake whose surface is not very disturbed or agitated but only slightly rippled by the wafting of some wind.

And finally, it can happen that, over the course of time, these surfaces change a little, or indeed some bend quite noticeably in a short time, even if this would be only when a comet approached them. In this way, after a long time, many stars seem to change place slightly without changing size or change size slightly without changing place; some of them even quite suddenly begin to appear or disappear, as it was observed in the real world.

As for the planets and comets in the same heaven as the sun, knowing that the parts of the third element they are composed of are so large or many are so joined together that they can resist the action of light, it is easy to understand that they must appear by means of the rays the sun sends toward them, which are reflected from there toward the earth. In the same way opaque or obscure objects in a room can be seen there by means of the rays that a flaming torch illuminating them sends toward them, which are reflected from there toward the eyes of the observers. In addition, the rays of the sun have a very remarkable advantage over those of a torch, in that their force is conserved or even increased more and more as they move away from the sun, until they have reached the external surface of its heaven, because all the matter of that heaven tends there. Instead, the rays of a torch weaken as they move away, in proportion to the size of the spherical surfaces they illuminate, and even somewhat more, because of the resistance of the air through which they pass. As a result, the objects close to this torch are noticeably more illuminated than those far from it; and the lowest planets are not, in the same proportion, more illuminated by the sun, than the highest ones, nor even than the comets, which are incomparably more distant.

Now experience shows us that the same thing also happens in the real world. And yet I do not believe that it is possible to account for it, if we suppose that light is anything other than an action or disposition in the objects, such as I explained it. I say an action or disposition, for,

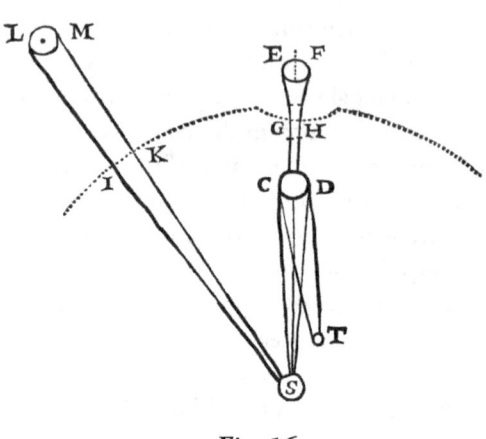

Fig. 16

if you attended to what I just showed, that if the space where the sun is were completely void, the parts of its heaven would not fail to tend toward the eyes of the observers in the same way as when they are pushed by its matter, and even with almost as much force, you can well judge that it hardly needs to have any action in itself, nor even to be anything but a pure space, for it to appear as we see it—something you might have taken earlier to be a quite paradoxical proposition. Moreover, the motion these planets have around their center is what causes them to twinkle, but much less strongly and in a different way than fixed stars do; and because the moon is deprived of this motion, it does not twinkle at all.

As for the comets not in the same heaven as the sun, they cannot nearly send as many rays toward the earth as they could than if they were in the same heaven, not even when they are ready to enter it. Consequently, they cannot be seen by people, unless perhaps when their size is extraordinary. This is because most of the rays the sun sends toward them are spread here and there and, as it were, dissipated by the refraction they undergo in the part of the firmament through which they pass. For example, whereas comet CD receives from the sun, marked S, all the rays between lines SC and SD and sends back all those between lines CT and DT toward the earth, we must consider that comet EF receives from the same sun only the rays between lines SGE and SHF because, since they pass much more easily from S to surface GH, which I take to be part of the firmament they cannot pass beyond, their refraction there must be very great and strongly outward. This diverts many of them to go toward comet EF, given mainly that this surface is curved inward toward the sun, as you know it should curve when a comet approaches it. But even if it were quite flat or curved in the other direction, most of the rays the sun would send to it would not fail to be prevented by refraction, if not from going as far as it, at least from returning from there to earth. For example, supposing the part of firmament IK to be a portion of a sphere whose center is at point S, rays SIL and SKM should not bend there at all going toward comet LM; but, on the other hand, they should bend a lot returning from there toward the earth, so they can only reach the earth very weakly and in very small quantity. Beyond that, since this can only happen when the comet is still far enough from the heaven containing the sun (for otherwise, if it were close to it, it would cause its surface to curve inward), its distance also impedes it from receiving as many rays as when it is ready to enter the heaven. As for the rays it receives from the fixed star in the center of the heaven containing it, it cannot send them back toward the earth, any more than the new moon can send back those of the sun.

But what is most remarkable regarding these comets is a certain refraction of their rays usually causing some of them to appear with the form of a tail or hair around them. You will easily understand, if you cast your eyes on this figure, where S is the sun, C a comet, EBG the sphere which, according to what was said earlier, is composed of the largest and least agitated parts of the second element, and DA the circle described by the annual motion of the earth. Consider that the ray coming from C toward B passes directly toward point A but in addition begins to widen at point B and to divide

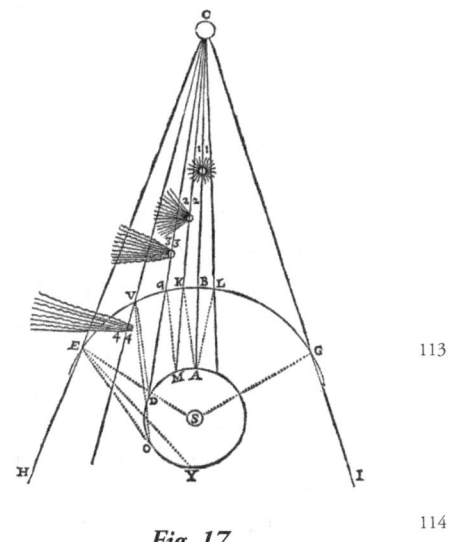

Fig. 17

into several other rays extending here and there in all directions. As a result, each of them is that much weaker as it deviates more from BA, in the middle, which is the principal and strongest ray. And then, when ray CE is at point E, it begins to grow larger and to divide into many others, such as EH, EY, and ES; but the principal and strongest of these is EH, and the weakest ES. In the same way, CG passes principally from G toward I, but in addition it also diverges from S and toward all the spaces between GI and GS. Finally, all the other rays that can be imagined between rays CE, CB, and CG hold in various degree to the nature of each of them, depending on their closeness to them. To this I could add that they should be bent a bit toward the sun; but this is not fully necessary for my purposes, and I often omit many things to make those I am explaining that much simpler and easier.

Now, supposing this refraction, it is manifest that, when the earth is at A, not only should people on the earth be caused to see the body of comet C by ray BA, but also rays LA, KA, and the like, which come to their eyes more weakly than BA, should cause to appear a crown or hair of light spread out in all directions around it (as you see at the place marked 11), at least if they are strong enough to be perceived. They often can be strong enough, coming from comets, which we suppose to be very large, but not coming from planets, nor even fixed stars, which should be imagined smaller.

It is also manifest that, when the earth is at M, and the comet appears by means of ray CKM, its hair should appear by means of QM, and all the other rays tending toward M, so that it extends farther than before toward the part opposite to the sun, and less far, or not at all, toward the person looking at it, as you see here at 22. And thus, always appearing longer and longer on the side opposite to the sun, to the extent the earth is farther from point A, it gradually loses the shape of hair, and is transformed into a long tail, which the comet trails behind it. For example, when the earth is at D, rays QD and VD make it appear as it is at 33. And when the earth is at o, rays Vo, Eo, and the like make it appear still longer; and finally, when the earth is at Y, we can no longer see the comet because of the interposition of the sun, but rays VY, EY, and the like do not fail to cause its tail to appear in a V-shape or a fire jet, as here at 44. And it should be noted that, since sphere EBG is not always exactly round, nor also are any of the others it contains, as it is easy to judge from what we explained, these tails or fire jets should not always appear exactly straight, nor entirely in the same plane as the sun.

As for the refraction which is the cause of all this, I confess that its nature is very peculiar and very different from all those commonly observed elsewhere. But you will not fail to see clearly that it should take place in the way I just described to you if you consider that ball H, being pushed toward I, also pushes toward I all those below it down to K; but the latter, being surrounded by several other smaller balls, such as 4, 5, and 6, only pushes 5 toward I; and yet it pushes 4 toward L and 6 toward M, and so on, such that it pushes the middle one, 5, much harder than the others, 4 and 6, and similar ones on the sides. In the same way, ball N, being pushed toward L, pushes the small balls 1, 2, and 3, one toward L, the other toward I, and the other toward M, but with this difference, that it pushes 1 the most strongly of all, and not 2, the middle one. Moreover, the small balls 1, 2, 3, 4, etc., being thus all pushed at the same time by the other balls N, P, H, P, impede one another from being able to go toward L and M as easily as toward the middle, I. Thus, if the whole space L I M were full of similar small balls, the rays of their action would be distributed there in the same way as I said are those of the comets within sphere E B G.

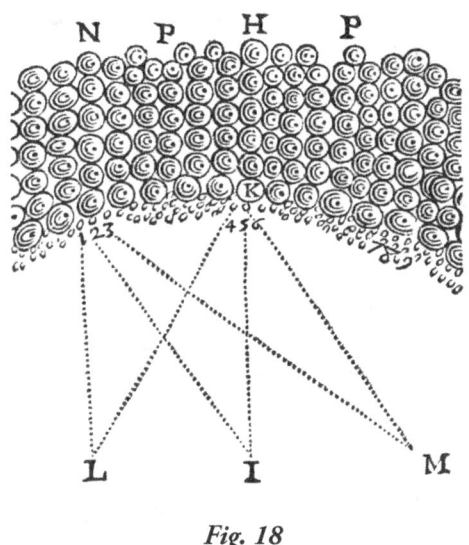

Fig. 18

If you object to this that the inequality between balls N, P, H, P, and 1, 2, 3, 4, etc., is much greater than the one I supposed between the parts of the second element composing sphere E B G and the ones immediately below them toward the sun, I reply that the only consequence to be drawn from this is that less refraction must occur in sphere E B G than in the one composed of balls 1, 2, 3, 4, etc.; but since there is in turn some inequality between the parts of the second element immediately below this sphere E B G and those still lower toward the sun, this refraction increases more and more as the rays penetrate farther. Thus, when the rays reach the sphere of earth D A F, the refraction may well be as great, or even greater than that of the action by which the small balls 1, 2, 3, 4, etc., are pushed. For it is very likely that the parts of the second element toward the sphere of earth D A F are not any smaller in comparison with those toward sphere E B G than are those balls 1, 2, 3, 4, etc., in comparison with the other balls N, P, H, P.

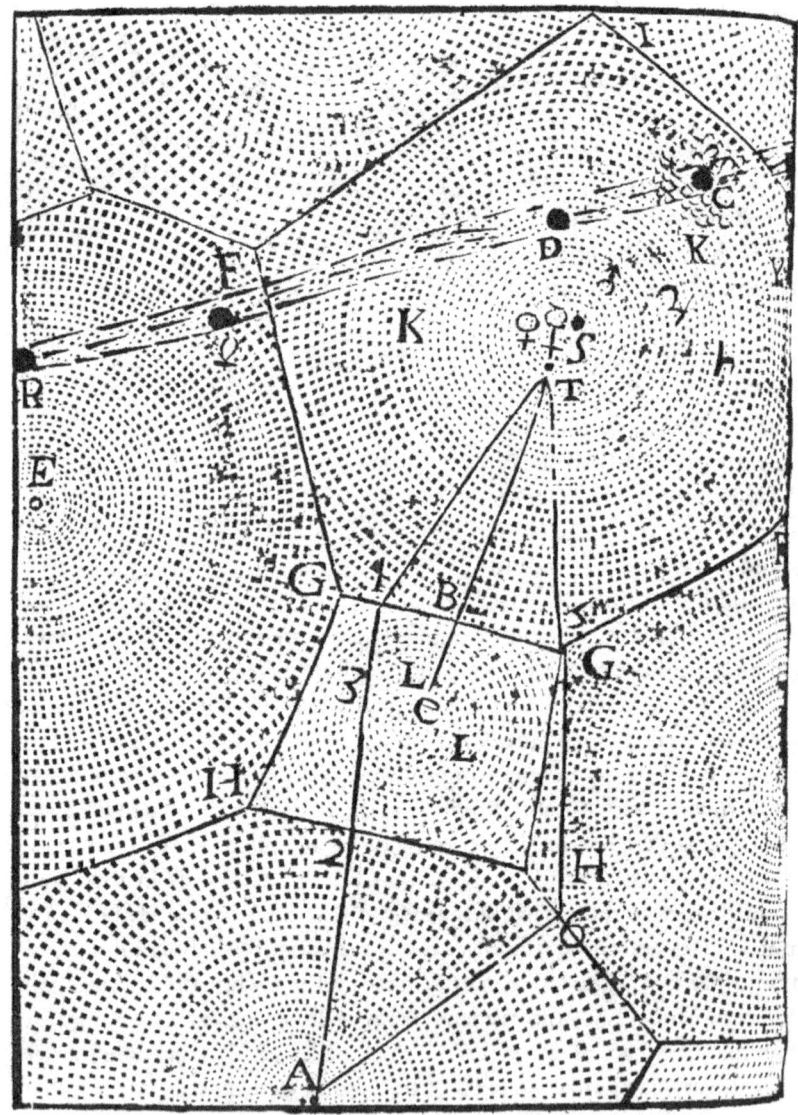

Fig. 2 of The World *(Le Monde, 1664)*
Descartes's world, showing the sun at the center of its vortex, with the planets, including the earth, being carried around it, and a comet going across the vortices.

Part II

Man[1]

Section 1. The Machine of the Body[2]

Like us, these people[3] will be composed of a soul and a body. I must first describe to you the body by itself, and afterward the soul, also by itself, and finally, I must show you how these two natures should be joined and united to compose people resembling us.

I suppose the body to be nothing other than a statue or an earthen machine, formed expressly by God to make it as much as possible like us, so that, not only does he give it externally the color and shape of all our bodily members, he also puts inside it all the parts required to make it walk, eat, breathe, and ultimately imitate all those of our functions that can be imagined to proceed from matter and to depend only on the arrangement of organs.

We see clocks, artificial fountains, mills, and other similar machines, which, though made entirely by people, do not lack the power to move of themselves in many different ways; and it seems to me I could not imagine so many kinds of motions in this machine, which I am supposing to be made by the hands of God, nor attribute to it so much artistry, that you do not have reason to think there may not have been even more.

Now, I will not stop to describe the bones, nerves, muscles, veins, arteries, stomach, liver, spleen, heart, brain, nor all the other different parts of which the machine must be composed. For I suppose them to be wholly like the parts of our body with the same names that some learned

---

1. Claude Clerselier indicates that "Man" was originally chapter 18 of *The World or Treatise on Light*. It was published separately as the *Treatise on Man* in Latin translation (*De Homine*, Leyden, 1662), and in French (*L'Homme*, Paris, 1664 and 1677). Chapters 16 and 17 are unknown.

2. The titles and division into five sections are suggested by Clerselier, who also suggests a further division into 106 articles (see AT XI, 203–9).

3. That is, the people of the new world Descartes is describing.

anatomist may show you, at least those large enough to be perceived, if you do not already know them well enough by yourself. And, as for the parts too small to be visible, I will be able to make them more easily and clearly known to you by speaking of the motions depending on them, so that I only need here to explain these motions in their proper order and tell you by the same means which of our functions they represent.

First, food is digested in the stomach of this machine by the force of certain liquids that, gliding among their parts, separate, agitate, and heat them, just as ordinary water does with those of quicklime or acid those of metals. Moreover, these liquids, since they are brought from the heart very quickly through the arteries, as I will soon explain, cannot fail to be very hot. And indeed, food is usually such that it can be corrupted and heated on its own, just as new hay does in the barn when it is confined there before it is dry.

You should know that the agitation given to the small particles of food as they are heated, combined with the agitation of the stomach and bowels containing them, as well as the arrangement of the small fibers of which these bowels are composed, cause these particles, to the extent they are digested, to descend gradually toward the conduit through which the coarsest particles must exit. In the meanwhile, the subtlest and most agitated of them encounter here and there infinitely many little holes through which they flow into the branches of a large vein carrying them toward the liver, and into other branches carrying them elsewhere, without there being anything but the smallness of these holes to separate them from the coarser particles. This is just as, when you shake flour in a sieve, the purest flour flows through the sieve, and nothing but the smallness of the holes through which it passes prevents the bran from following it.

These subtler particles of food, being unequal and still imperfectly mixed together, compose a liquid that would remain quite turbulent and whitish, if part of it did not immediately intermingle with the mass of blood contained in the branches of the vein called portal (which receives this liquid from the intestines), in those of the vein called vena cava (which conducts it toward the heart), and in the liver, as if in a single vessel.

Similarly, you should note here that the pores of the liver are so arranged that, when this liquid enters it, it becomes more subtle and refined, taking on the color and acquiring the form of blood there, just as the white juice of black grapes is converted into light red wine when it is left to ripen on the grape sediment.

Now this blood thus contained in the veins has only one obvious passage by which it can exit, namely, the one conducting it into the right cavity of the heart. And you should know that the flesh of the heart contains in its pores one of those fires without light of which I spoke earlier, rendering it so hot and fiery that, to the extent blood enters either of the two chambers or cavities there, it quickly inflates and dilates. Similarly, you can observe what happens to the blood or milk of any animal if you pour it drop by drop into a very hot receptacle. The fire in the heart of the machine I am describing to you serves no other purpose than to dilate, heat, and subtilize the blood falling continuously drop by drop through a tube, from the vena cava into the cavity on its right side, from where it is exhaled into the lung, and from the vein of the lung anatomists call *venous artery* into its other cavity, from where it is distributed throughout the body.

The flesh of the lung is so rare and soft, and always so refreshed by the air of respiration that, as the vapors of the blood issuing from the right cavity of the heart enter in through the artery anatomists call *arterial vein*, they are thickened and reconverted into blood. Then, drop by drop, this blood falls into the left cavity of the heart where, if the vapors entered without being thus thickened again, they would be inadequate to nourish the fire found there.

And so you see that respiration, whose sole use in this machine is to thicken these vapors, is no less necessary for maintaining this fire as it is in us for preserving our life, at least in those of us who are fully formed, for infants still in their mothers' wombs cannot draw any fresh air by respiration and have two conduits that make up for this lack: one through which the blood from the vena cava passes into the vein called artery, and the other through which the vapors, or the rarefied blood of the artery called vein, are exhaled and go into the great artery.[4] And, as for animals with no lungs at all, they have only one cavity in their heart or, if they have several, they are all consecutive to one another.

The pulse, or beating of the arteries, depends on eleven small membranes, which, like so many little doors, close and open the orifices to the four vessels that open into the two cavities of the heart. For, when a beat

---

4. The aorta. We are keeping the terms Descartes uses since he himself keeps them, although he notes that some of them are wrong. See also Descartes's *Discourse on Method*, Part V, AT VI, 47 (Appendix B).

ceases and another is about to begin, the little doors at the entrances to the two arteries are tightly shut, and those at the entrances to the two veins are open, so that two drops of blood cannot but fall immediately through these two veins, one into each cavity of the heart. These drops of blood, being rarefied and suddenly extending into an incomparably greater space than the one they previously occupied, then push shut the little doors at the orifices of the two veins, preventing in this way any more blood from dropping into the heart; they then push open the doors of the two arteries through which they enter quickly and with force, thus causing the heart and all the body's arteries to inflate at the same time. But immediately afterward, this rarefied blood condenses again or penetrates other parts of the body; and thus, the heart and arteries are deflated, the little doors at the two orifices of the arteries are shut again, and those at the orifices to the two veins are reopened to admit two more drops of blood, which cause the heart and arteries to inflate again, exactly as before.

Knowing the cause of the pulse, it is easy to understand that it is not so much the blood contained in the veins of this machine newly coming from its liver, as the one in its arteries already distilled in its heart, which can attach to its other parts and serve to replace what the continual agitation and the various actions of the other bodies surrounding these parts detach from them and sends away. For the blood in the veins always flows gradually from their extremities toward the heart (and the arrangement of certain little doors, or valves, the anatomists noted in several places along the veins should persuade you sufficiently that the same thing happens in us). On the other hand, blood in the arteries is pushed out of the heart with force, and in separate little spurts, toward their extremities. Thus, it can easily come to join and unite with all its members, and in this way, can maintain them or even make them grow, if the machine represents the body of a person so disposed.

For, at the moment the arteries inflate, the small parts of the blood they contain will randomly strike the roots of certain little fibers which, emerging from the extremities of the little branches of these arteries, make up bones, flesh, membranes, nerves, the brain, and all the solid members, depending on the different ways they are joined or intertwined; and thus they have the force to push the fibers forward a bit and to replace them. Then, at the moment the arteries deflate, each of these parts stops in its place, and in this way alone, it is joined and united with the part it touches, according to what was said earlier.

Now, if our machine represents the body of an infant, its matter will be so tender, and its pores so easily enlarged, that the parts of the blood entering thus into the composition of the solid members will generally be a little coarser than those they replace. It can even happen that two or three together will succeed only one, which causes growth. But in the meanwhile, the matter of its members will harden gradually, so that after a few years, its pores will not be able to enlarge as much; and so, ceasing to grow, the machine will represent the body of an older person.

Moreover, only a very few parts of the blood can be united every time to the solid members in the way I just explained; most of them return into the veins from the extremities of the arteries, which in many places are joined to those of the veins. And perhaps some parts also pass out of the veins to nourish some of the members, but most of them return to the heart, and from there go into the arteries again, in such a way that the motion of the blood in the body is just a perpetual circulation.

In addition, some of the parts of the blood go to the spleen and others to the gall bladder; some return to the stomach and bowels from the spleen and gall as well as directly from the arteries, where they act as acids to aid in the digestion of food. And because they are carried there from the heart almost at once through the arteries, they never fail to be very hot, which enables their vapors to rise easily through the gullet toward the mouth, where they compose the saliva. Some also flow out as urine through the flesh of the kidneys, or as sweat and other excrements throughout the skin. In all these places, only the position, shape, or smallness of the pores through which they pass allows some to go through rather than others and keeps the rest of the blood from following, just as you can see different sieves which, being pierced in different ways, serve to separate different grains from one another.

But what must be noted here mainly is that all the most energetic, strongest, and most subtle parts of this blood proceed to the cavities of the brain, inasmuch as the arteries carrying them there are those coming from the heart in the straightest line; and, as you know, all moving bodies tend as much as possible to continue their motion in a straight line.

Consider, for example, heart A [*Fig. 1*], and note that, when the blood is forced from it through opening B, all its parts tend toward C, where the cavities of the brain are located; but since the passage is not large enough to carry all of them there, the weakest are turned back by the stronger, which in this way proceed there alone.

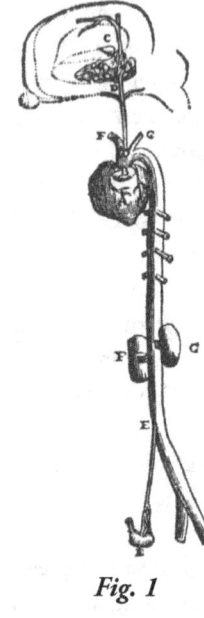

Fig. 1

You can also note in passing that, other than those entering the brain, there are no stronger or more lively parts than those going to the vessels destined for generation. For, if those with the force to reach D, for example, cannot go farther toward C because there is not enough room for all of them there, they return to E rather than to F or G, insofar as the passage is straighter there. Beyond this, I could perhaps show you how, from the humor gathering at E, another machine like this one can be formed, but I do not wish to go further into this matter.

As for the parts of blood penetrating as far as the brain, they serve not only to nourish and sustain its substance, but chiefly also to produce a certain very subtle wind, or rather a very lively and pure flame we call *animal spirits*. For we must understand that the arteries bringing them from the heart, after being divided into an infinity of small branches making up the small tissues stretched like tapestries at the base of the cavities of the brain, collect around a certain little *gland* situated about the middle of the brain's substance, just at the entrance to its cavities; the arteries there have many little holes through which the most subtle parts of the blood can flow into this gland, but these holes are so narrow that they refuse any passage to the larger parts.

You should also know that these arteries do not stop there, but several being gathered into one, they rise straight up and enter that great vessel which, like Euripus, bathes the whole external surface of the brain. Moreover, it should be noted that the coarsest parts of the blood can lose much of their agitation in the bends of the small tissues through which they pass, inasmuch as they have the power to push the smallest among them, and so transfer some of it to them; but the smaller ones cannot lose their motion in the same way, especially since their agitation is increased by what the larger parts transfer to them and because there are no other bodies around them to which they can so easily transfer theirs.

From this it is easy to conceive that when the coarser ones rise straight up to the external surface of the brain where they provide nourishment for its substance, they cause the smallest and more agitated parts to be diverted and all of them to enter this gland, which must be imagined as a very abundant spring from which they flow at the same time in all directions into the cavities of the brain. And thus, without further preparation or change, other than being separated from the coarser parts and retaining the extreme speed that the heat of the heart gave them, they cease to have the form of blood and are called animal spirits.

Section 2. How the Machine of the Body Moves

Now, as these spirits enter the cavities of the brain, they pass from there into the pores in its substance, and from these pores into the nerves. There, depending on where they enter, or even only on where they tend to enter, in greater or lesser degree, into some nerves rather than into others, they have the force to change the shape of the muscles in which these nerves are inserted, and by this means to move all the members. In this way, you may have seen in the grottos and fountains of the royal gardens, that only the force of the moving water as it emerges from its source is enough to move various machines and even to make them play certain instruments or pronounce certain words, according to the different arrangements of the tubes through which the water is conducted.

And truly, the nerves of the machine I am describing can very well be compared to the tubes of the machinery of these fountains, its muscles and its tendons to various other devices and springs serving to move them, its animal spirits to the water that sets them in motion, of which the heart is the source and the cavities of the brain the openings.[5] Moreover, respiration and other such actions as natural and normal to it, that depend on the course of the spirits, are like the motions of a clock or mill that the regular flow of water can render continuous. External objects, which by their mere presence act on its sense organs and by this means determine them to move in several different ways according to the disposition of the parts of its brain, are like visitors who, entering some of the grottos of these fountains, unintentionally cause the motions occurring in their presence. For they cannot enter without stepping on certain tiles of the pavement so arranged that, for example, if they approach a Diana

---

5. The word we are translating as "openings" here and below is *les regards*. It is a common French word, referring to looks or glances, but here it is used as a technical term for the access points from which one can observe a machine's inner works, that is, its wheels, cogs, tubes, and other devices. In hydraulics, it refers to a reservoir where the controls and faucets to distribute or raise the flow of water are placed.

bathing, they cause her to hide in the reeds, and if they move forward to pursue her, they cause a Neptune to advance and threaten them with his trident, or if they turn in some other direction, they cause a sea monster to come out and squirt water in their faces—or similar other things according to the whim of the engineers who constructed the fountains. And finally, when the *rational soul* will be present in this machine, it will have its principal seat in the brain, and it will be there like the controller of fountains who must be stationed at the openings to where all the tubes of these machines proceed, if he wants to excite, prevent, or change their motions in some way.

But so that you may understand all this distinctly, I wish first to tell you of the fabric of the nerves and muscles, and to show you how, from the sole fact that the spirits in the brain present themselves to enter into some nerves, they have the force to move a member at the same instant. Then, having touched briefly on respiration and such other simple and ordinary motions, I will say how external objects act upon the sense organs. After this, I will explain in detail everything occurring in the cavities and pores of the brain, what path animal spirits take there, and which of our functions this machine can imitate by their means. For, if I began with the brain and only followed the course of the spirits, as I did with the blood, it seems to me my discourse would be far less clear.

Hence, observe here, for example, nerve A [*Fig. 2*] whose external membrane is like a large tube containing several other small tubes *b, c, k, l,* etc., composed from a thinner internal membrane; and observe also that these two membranes are continuous with the two, K and L, covering brain M N O.

Also observe that in each of these little tubes, there is something like a marrow composed of several very thin fibers coming from the very substance of brain N whose extremities end, one at its internal surface facing its cavities, and the other at the membranes and flesh on which the tube containing them terminates. But, because this marrow is not used to move the members, it is enough for now that you understand it does not so completely fill the small tubes containing it, such that the animal spirits would not find enough place there to flow easily from the brain

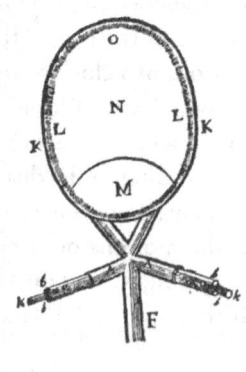

Fig. 2

into the muscles, where these small tubes, which must be thought of as so many little nerves, proceed.

Next, observe how the tube, or tiny nerve *bf* [Fig. 3, as well as Fig. 3a and 3b], proceeds to muscle D, which I suppose to be one of those moving the eye, and how it divides into several branches composed of a loose membrane that can extend, or widen and shrink, according to the quantity of animal spirits entering or exiting it. Those branches or filaments are so arranged that, when animal spirits enter, they cause the whole body of the muscle to inflate and shorten, thus pulling the eye to which it is attached, whereas, in contrast, when they exit, the muscle deflates and lengthens again.

Moreover, observe that in addition to tube *bf*, there is another, namely *ef*, through which animal spirits can enter muscle D, and still another, namely *dg*, through which they can exit. And in just the same way, muscle E, which I suppose serves to move the eye in the opposite direction to the previous muscle, receives animal spirits from the brain through tube *cg*, and from muscle D through *dg*, and sends them back to D through *ef*. And observe that there is no evident passage through which the spirits contained in muscles D and E can exit, except to go into each other; however, because their parts are very small, and indeed because they are constantly made smaller by the force of their agitation, some always escape through the membranes and flesh of these muscles, while others also return through tubes *bf* and *cg*.

Finally observe that, at the juncture of tubes *bf* and *ef* [Fig. 4], there is a certain small membrane H*fi* separating these two tubes and serving as a door. It has two flaps, H and *i*, so arranged that, when the animal spirits tending downward from *b* toward H are stronger than those tending upward from *e* toward *i*, they push down and open this membrane, thus allowing those in muscle E to flow promptly toward D. But when those tending upward from *e* toward *i* are stronger or even as strong as the others, they move upward and close membrane H*fi*, thus preventing themselves from exiting muscle E; however, if they are not strong enough to push it from either side, it naturally remains open. Finally, if at times the spirits contained in muscle D tend to exit through *dfe* or *dfb*, flap H can be extended and block their passage. Similarly, between tubes *cg* and *dg*, there is a small membrane or valve *g*, like the previous one, that remains open naturally and can be closed by the spirits coming from tube *dg* and opened by those coming from *cg*.

Fig. 3

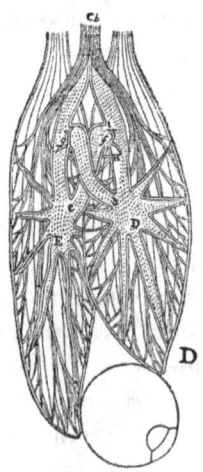

Fig. 3a

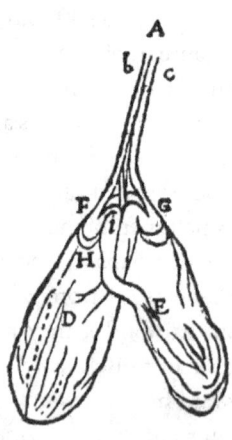

Fig. 3b

These two figures seem to be by Descartes himself: the first is said to be Descartes's by Clerselier in his Preface of the 1664 French edition (L'Homme); and the second, printed in the 1662 Latin edition (De Homine), is accompanied by the caption, "Figure of the muscles following Descartes's original sketch."

As a result, it is easy to understand that, if the animal spirits in the brain [*Fig. 3*] tend not to flow, or hardly at all, through tubes *bf* and *cg*, the two small membranes or valves *f* and *g* remain open, and thus muscles D and E are loose and inactive, to the extent that the animal spirits they contain pass freely from one muscle into the other, coursing from *e* through

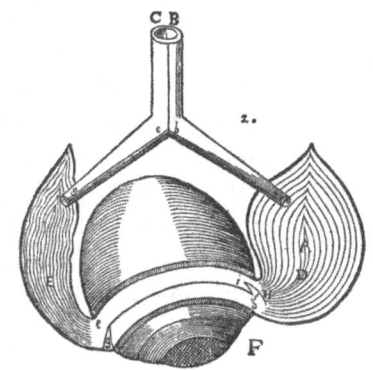

Fig. 4

f toward *d*, and vice versa from *d* through *g* toward *e*. But if the spirits in the brain tend to enter tubes *bf* and *cg* with some force and this force is equal on both sides, they immediately close passages *g* and *f* and inflate muscles D and E as much as possible, thereby making them stop and hold the eye firmly in its position.

But if these spirits coming from the brain tend to flow with greater force through *bf* than through *cg*, they close small membrane *g* and open *f*; they do this to a greater or lesser degree depending on how strongly they strike it. In this way, the spirits contained in muscle E proceed to muscle D through channel *ef*; they do this with greater or lesser speed depending on how open membrane *f* is. As a result, muscle D, which these spirits cannot exit, contracts and E elongates; and thus, the eye is turned toward D. On the other hand, if the spirits in the brain tend to flow through *cg* with more force than through *bf*, they close little membrane *f* and open *g*, such that the spirits of muscle D immediately return through channel *dg* to muscle E, which in this way contracts and turns the eye to its side.

For you know well that these spirits, being like a wind or very subtle flame, cannot fail to flow very quickly from one muscle to another as soon as they find some passage, even though no other force propels them there than the inclination they possess to continue their motion, according to the laws of nature. And you know, further, that even though they are very mobile and subtle, they still have the strength to inflate and tighten the muscles in which they are enclosed, just as the air in a balloon hardens it and stretches the membranes containing it.

Now you can easily apply what I just said about nerve A and the two muscles D and E to all the other muscles and nerves, and thus to understand how the machine I am describing can be moved in all the same ways as our bodies, solely by the force of the animal spirits flowing from the brain into the nerves. For you can imagine, for each motion and its opposite, two little nerves or tubes, such as *bf* and *cg*, and two others, such as *cg* and *ef*, and two little doors or valves, such as H*fi* and *g*.

And, as for the ways these tubes are inserted into the muscles, although they vary in a thousand ways, it is nevertheless not difficult to judge what they are by knowing what anatomy can teach you about the external shape and the use of each muscle.

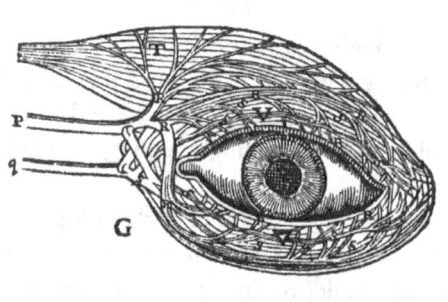

Fig. 5

For knowing, for example, that the eyelids are moved by two muscles [*Fig. 5*], of which one, namely T, serves only to open the upper eyelid, and the other, namely V, serves alternately to open and close both eyelids, it is easy to think that they receive the spirits through two tubes such as *p*R and *q*s; and that *p*R, one of these two tubes, proceeds to both muscles, and the other, *q*s, to only one of them. In addition, branches R and s, being, as it were, inserted in the same way into muscle V, nevertheless produce two completely opposite effects, because of the different arrangement of their branches or filaments; this will suffice for understanding the others as well.

And indeed, it is not difficult to judge from the foregoing that animal spirits can cause motions in all the members where nerves terminate, although there are many in which anatomists did not notice any visible nerves, such as the pupil of the eye, the heart, liver, gall bladder, spleen, and the like.

Now, to understand in particular how this machine breathes, consider that muscle *d* [*Fig. 6*] is one of those used to raise its chest or lower its diaphragm, and that muscle E is its opposite; consider also that the animal spirits in the cavity of the brain marked *m*, flowing through the pore or small channel marked *n*, which by its nature remains always open, proceed first to tube BF where, lowering little membrane F, they cause spirits from muscle E to come and inflate muscle *d*.

Consider next that there are certain membranes around this muscle *d* pressing on it more and more as it inflates and so arranged that, before all the spirits of muscle E can pass through it, they are stopped in their course, causing them to be regorged, as it were, through tube BF. The result is that those from channel *n* are diverted; in this way, they proceed to tube *cg*, which they open at the same time, causing muscle E to inflate and muscle *d* to deflate. They continue to do this for as long as they are subject to the impetuosity of the spirits contained in muscle *d* which, pressed by

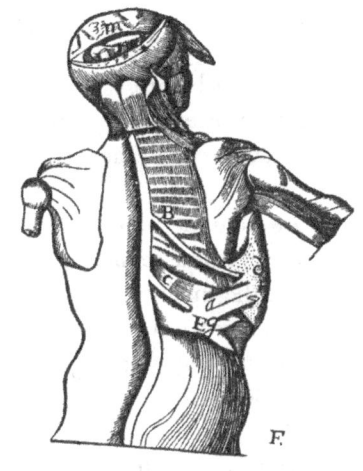

Fig. 6

the surrounding membranes, tend to exit from it. Then, when this impetuosity no longer has any force, they resume their course through tube BF, and thus continuously inflate and deflate these two muscles alternatively. You should also conclude this of the other muscles serving the same effect and think they are all so disposed that, when ones such as *d* are inflated, the space containing the lungs widens, causing the air to enter, just as it does when one opens a bellows. And when the contrary happens, this space shrinks, causing the air to exit again.

To understand also how this machine swallows the food at the back of its mouth, consider that muscle *d* is one of those raising the root of its tongue, keeping open the passage through which the air it breathes must pass to enter the lung; and muscle E is its opposite, serving to close this passage and by the same means to open the one through which the food in its mouth must descend into its stomach, or rather to raise the tip of its tongue pushing it there. Moreover, the animal spirits coming from brain cavity *m* through pore or little channel *n*, which naturally always remains open, proceed straight into tube BF, by means of which they inflate muscle *d*. This muscle remains thus constantly inflated as long as there is no food at the back of the mouth that can press on it; but it is so disposed that, when food is there, the spirits it contains immediately overflow through tube BF and cause those coming through channel *n* to enter tube *cg* into muscle E through tube *cg*, to where the spirits also proceed: and thus the throat opens and the food descends into the stomach; immediately after this, the spirits from channel *n* resume their course through BF as before.

Given this example, you can also understand how this machine can sneeze, yawn, cough, and make the motions necessary to reject various other excrements.

Next, to understand how external objects striking the sense organs can incite the machine to move its members in a thousand different ways, consider that the small fibers, which I already said come from the innermost part of its brain and compose the marrow of its nerves, are so arranged in every part serving as an organ of sense that they can very easily be moved by the objects of that sense. When they are moved, with however little force, they simultaneously pull the parts of the brain from which they come, and by the same means, open the entrances to certain pores in the internal surface of the brain. The animal spirits in the cavities of the brain begin immediately to make their way through these pores into the nerves and thus into the muscles, causing motions in this machine quite like those we are naturally incited to make when our senses are impacted in the same way.

As, for example, if fire A is near foot B [*Fig. 7*], the small parts of this fire, which as you know, move very rapidly, have the force to displace the area of skin they touch, and in this way, pulling small fiber *cc* you see attached to it, they simultaneously open the entrance to pore *de* at which this small fiber ends, just as, pulling on one end of a rope causes the bell hanging at the other end to ring at the same time.

Now the entrance to pore or small duct *de* being thus open, the animal spirits from cavity F enter and are carried through it, some to the muscles serving to pull the foot away from the fire, some into the muscles serving to turn the eyes and head to look at the

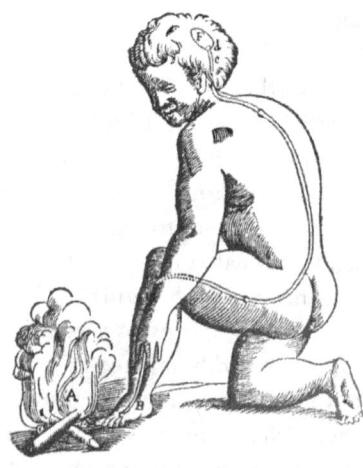

Fig. 7

fire, and some to the muscles serving to move the hands and turn the whole body to protect itself.

But they can also be carried by the same conduit *d e* into several other muscles. And before pausing to explain more precisely how animal spirits follow their course through the pores of the brain and how these pores are arranged, I wish to speak here specifically about all the senses, such as they exist in this machine, and tell you how they relate to our own.

Section 3. The External Senses of This Machine and How They Are Related to Our External Senses

Note first that there are a great number of small fibers like *cc* beginning to separate from one another at the internal surface of the brain where they originate, spreading from there throughout the rest of its body where they serve as the organs of the sense of touch. For, even though external objects do not ordinarily touch the fibers, but touch the skin surrounding them, there is no more reason to think of the skin as the organs of sense than there is to think of gloves as the sense organ when we are handling something while wearing gloves.

And note that even though the fibers I speak of are very thin, they extend securely from the brain to the most distant members without there being anything in between breaking them or preventing their action through pressure, even though these members bend in a thousand different ways. The little tubes containing the fibers carry the animal spirits to the muscles, and these spirits, always inflating these tubes somewhat, prevent them from being pressed and keep the fibers as taut as possible along the path from the brain where they originate to where they terminate.

Now I claim that when God will unite a rational soul to this machine, as I intend to assert later on, he will place its principal seat in the brain and make its nature such that the soul will have various sensations according to the different ways the entrances of the pores in the internal surface of this brain are opened through the mediation of the nerves.

Thus, first, if the little fibers composing the marrow of these nerves are pulled with enough force that they break and separate from the part to which they were joined, so that the whole structure of the machine is in some way less intact, the motion they then cause in the brain will give the soul (to which it is important that its place of residence be preserved) an occasion to have the sensation of *pain*.

And if they are pulled by a force almost as great as the previous one, without however breaking or separating in any way from the parts to which they are attached, they will cause a motion in the brain, which, testifying to the good condition of the other members will give the soul an occasion to feel a certain bodily pleasure called *tickling*, and which, as you see, being very close to the pain in its cause, is quite opposite in its effect.

But if many of these little fibers are pulled together equally, they will make the soul feel the surface of the body touching the members where they terminate as *smooth*; and if the fibers are pulled unevenly, they will cause the soul to feel it as uneven and *rough*.

If they are only shaken slightly, separately from one another, as they are continually by the heat that the heart communicates to the other members, the soul will have no more sensation of this, any more than any other ordinary actions; but if this motion is increased or diminished in them by some unusual cause, its increase will cause the soul to have the sensation of *heat*, and its diminution a sensation of *cold*. And finally, according to the other various ways they are moved, they will cause the soul to sense all the other qualities belonging to touch in general, such as *humidity*, *dryness*, *heaviness*, and the like.

It should be noted that, as very fine and mobile as these fibers might be, they are not, however, so much so that they can transmit to the brain all the slightest actions in nature; the smallest ones they transmit are those from the coarsest particles of terrestrial bodies. Indeed, there may be some of these bodies whose particles, even though quite coarse, can slide against the small fibers so gently that they press against them or cut them completely without their action passing to the brain, just as there are certain drugs with the power to numb or even damage the members on which they are applied without causing us to have any sensation of them at all.

But the small fibers making up the marrow of the nerves of the tongue and serving as an organ of taste in this machine can be moved by slighter actions than those only serving for touch in general, because they are a bit finer, and the membranes covering them more tender.

Consider, for example, that they can be moved in four different ways, by the particles of salt, acidulous water, fresh water, and brandy, whose sizes and shapes I already explained,[6] and thus they can cause the soul

---

6. See *Meteors*, AT VI, 233–38, though Descartes might be referring to one of the missing chapters of *Le Monde*, chapters 16 or 17.

to sense four different kinds of tastes. To the extent the particles of salts are separated from one another and agitated by the action of saliva, they enter, pointed end foremost and without bending, into the pores in the skin of the tongue; those of acids flow through it diagonally, slicing or cutting its most tender parts while yielding to the coarsest; those of fresh water merely glide over it, without incising any of its parts or penetrating far into its pores; and finally those of brandy, being very small, penetrate the most of all and move with very great speed. From this, you can easily judge how the soul will be able to sense all the other sorts of tastes, if you consider in how many other ways the small particles of terrestrial bodies can act against the tongue.

But what must be noted here mainly is that the same small particles of food which, while in the mouth, can enter the pores of the tongue and excite the sensation of taste there, and while in the stomach, can pass into the blood and from there join and unite with all the members, indeed, only those tickling the tongue moderately, and in this way causing the soul to sense an agreeable taste, are entirely suited for this purpose.

For, just as particles of food that are too active or too inactive can only cause too sharp or too bland a taste, they are also too penetrating or too soft to enter into the composition of the blood and be used for the maintenance of some members. Moreover, some particles of food are overly large or so tightly joined to one another that they cannot be separated by the action of saliva; or they cannot penetrate into the pores of the tongue to act on the small nerve fibers used for taste there, except insofar as they may act on the other body parts used for touch in general; or they do not have pores within themselves where the small parts of the tongue, or at least those of the saliva with which it is moistened, can enter. Since such particles of food will not be able to cause the soul to sense any taste or flavor, they are usually unsuitable for being taken into the stomach.

147

And this is so generally true that often, as the stomach's temperament changes, the strength of the taste also changes, so that a food that usually seems agreeable in taste to the soul may even at times seem bland or bitter; the reason for this is that the saliva coming from the stomach, retaining the qualities of the humor abounding there, mixes with the small particles of food in the mouth and contributes much to their action.

The sense of *smell* also depends on many small fibers protruding from the base of the brain toward the nose below those two small hollowed-out parts, which anatomists have compared to the nipples of a woman's breasts.

148   These do not differ in any way from the nerves used for touch and taste, except that they do not exit the cavity of the head that contains the whole brain, and that they can be moved by even smaller terrestrial particles than the nerves of the tongue, both because they are a little finer, and also because they are more immediately touched by the objects that move them.

For you should know that when this machine breathes, the subtlest particles of air entering it through the nose penetrate through the pores of the bone called spongy, if not all the way to the cavities of the brain, at least to the space between the two membranes surrounding it; from there they can exit again through the palate. Reciprocally, when air leaves the chest, they can enter this space through the palate and exit through the nose. At the entrance to this space, the particles of air encounter the ends of the little fibers, which are uncovered, or covered only with an extremely thin membrane requiring little force to move.

149   You should also know that these pores are so arranged, and so narrow, that they admit to these small fibers no terrestrial particles coarser than those which, when speaking on this subject before, I called *odors*, except perhaps also some of the ones composing brandy, whose shape makes them very penetrating.

Finally, you should know that, among these extremely small terrestrial particles, which are always found in greater abundance in the air than in any of the other composite bodies, only those a little coarser or finer than the others, or which because of their shape are moved more or less easily, can give occasion to the soul for various sensations of odors. And indeed, only those in which these extremes are much moderated and tempered by one another, will make it have agreeable ones. As for the particles acting only in an ordinary way, they will not be sensed at all; and those acting with too much or too little force can only be unpleasant to it.

As for the small fibers serving as the organ for the sense of *hearing*, they do not need to be as fine as the previous ones. It is enough to think of them as being so arranged at the back of the ear cavities that they can easily be moved all together and in the same way by the small blows from the external air pushing a certain very fine membrane stretched at the entrance to these cavities, and that they can be touched only by the air under this membrane. For these little blows, passing to the brain through the intervention of these nerves, will give the soul an occasion to conceive the idea of sound.

150   And note that only one of them will be able to cause him to hear anything other than a dull noise, which ceases in a moment and varies

only in being more or less loud, depending on whether the ear is struck with more or less force; but when many follow one another, as we observe when strings vibrate and bells ring, then these little blows will make up a sound that the soul will judge sweeter or harsher, depending on how equal or unequal the blows are to one another; and it will judge the sound more acute or grave, depending on how quickly or slowly they are in following one another, so that, if they follow one another more quickly by a half, or a third, or a fourth, or a fifth, etc., they will compose a sound that the soul will judge more acute by an octave, a fifth, a fourth, or a major third, etc. And finally, several sounds mixed together will be harmonious or discordant, depending on the extent to which their relations are orderly, and the intervals between the small blows composing them are more or less equal.

As, for example [*Fig. 8*], if the divisions of lines A, B, C, D, E, F, G, H represent the little blows composing as many different sounds, it is easy to judge that those represented by lines G and H cannot be as sweet to the ear as the others, just as the rough parts of a stone are not as smooth to the touch as those of a well-polished mirror. And B must be considered to represent a pitch higher than A by an

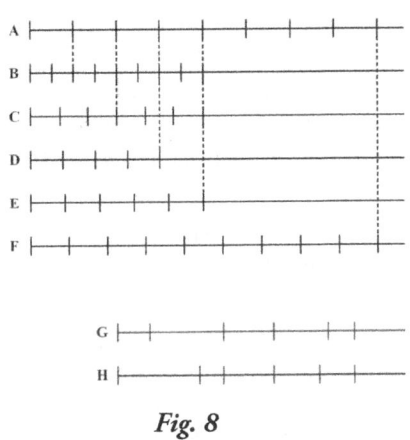

Fig. 8

octave, C by a fifth, D by a fourth, E by a major third, and F by a full major tone; and note that A and B joined together, or A B C, or A B D, or even A B C E are much more consonant than A and F, or A C D, or A D E, etc. This seems to me sufficient to show how the soul, when in the machine I am describing, will be able to enjoy a kind of music that follows all the same rules as ours, and even how it will be able to make it much more perfect, at least if we consider that it is not absolutely the sweetest things that are the most agreeable to the senses, but those titillate them in the best-tempered way, just as salt and vinegar are often more agreeable to the tongue than fresh water. And this is what makes music as receptive of thirds and sixths, and sometimes even of dissonances, as it is of unison, octaves, and fifths.

There remains the sense of *vision*, which I need to explain a little more precisely than the others because it is more useful to my topic. This sense depends in this machine, as in us, on two nerves, which must, without a doubt, be composed of several small fibers. These fibers are the most slender and the easiest to move, for their function is to report to the brain the different actions of the parts of the second element, which according to what was said earlier, will give occasion to the soul, when united with this machine, to conceive the different ideas of colors and light.

But because the structure of the eye also helps in producing this effect, I need to describe it here, and for greater ease, I will try to do so in a few words, leaving out quite deliberately several superfluous details noticed by anatomists.

A B C [*Fig. 9*] is a rather tough and thick membrane composing something like a round container, in which all other parts of the eye are contained. D E F is another, more slender membrane, stretched like a tapestry inside the previous one. G H I is the nerve whose small fibers H G and H I, spreading all around from H to G and I, completely cover the back of the eye. K, L, M are three kinds of extremely clear and transparent albumen, or humors, filling all the space contained inside these membranes, each having the shape represented here.[7]

In the first membrane, part B C B is transparent and a little more arched than the rest, and rays entering it are refracted toward the perpendicular. In the second membrane, the internal surface of part E F, which faces the back of the eye, is wholly black and obscure, having at its center a little round hole, called the *pupil*, which appears black in the middle of the eye when looked at from the outside. This hole is not always of the same size, because part E F of the membrane in which the hole floats freely in humor K, which is very liquid, seems to be like a little muscle, which enlarges or narrows as required under the direction of the brain.

The shape of the humor marked L, called the *crystalline humor*, is like the shape of lenses I described in the treatise on *Dioptrics*,[8] by means of which all the rays coming from a certain point are reassembled at another certain point; and its matter is less soft, or firmer, and consequently causes a greater refraction than that of the two other humors surrounding it.

---

7. See *Dioptrics*, AT VI, 106.
8. AT VI, 147–65.

E and N are small black fibers coming from within membrane D, E, F and embracing the crystalline humor. They are like so many small tendons by means of which its shape can be changed and made a little flatter or more arched, as needed. Finally, o, o are six or seven muscles attached to the eye on the outside, and can move it very easily and very quickly in all directions.

Now membrane BCB [*Fig. 9*], and the three humors K, L, M, being very clear and transparent, do not prevent light rays entering through the hole of the pupil from penetrating to the back of the eye where the nerve is, nor from acting as easily against it as if it were completely exposed. They serve to protect it against harm from air and other external bodies that could easily injure it, if they touched it, and they keep it so tender and delicate that it is not surprising it can be moved by actions so barely perceptible as are the ones I take here to be *colors*.

The curvature in the part of the first membrane marked BCB, and the refraction occurring there, cause the rays from objects located toward the sides of the eye to enter through the pupil. And thus, without the eye moving, the soul will be able to see a larger number of objects than it could otherwise. If, for example, ray PBKq did not bend at point B, it would be unable to pass between points F, F to reach the nerve.

The refraction occurring in the crystalline humor serves to make vision stronger and overall more distinct. For you should understand that the shape of this humor is so composed with regard to the refractions occurring in other parts of the eye and to the distance of objects, that when the vision is trained on a particular point of an object, it causes all the rays coming from this point and entering the eye through hole of the pupil, to reassemble at another point at the back of the eye. They assemble at precisely one part of the nerve there, and by the same means, any of the other rays entering the eye are prevented from touching the same part of this nerve.

For example [*Fig. 10*], when the eye is so arranged to look at point R, the arrangement of the crystalline humor makes all the rays RNS, RLS, etc., assemble exactly at point S, and by the same means prevents any of those coming from points T and X, etc., from arriving there. For it also assembles all those from point T around point V, those from point X around point Y, and so on. Whereas if there were no refraction in this eye, object R would send only one of its rays to point S, and the others would spread here and there throughout space VY; and in the same way, points

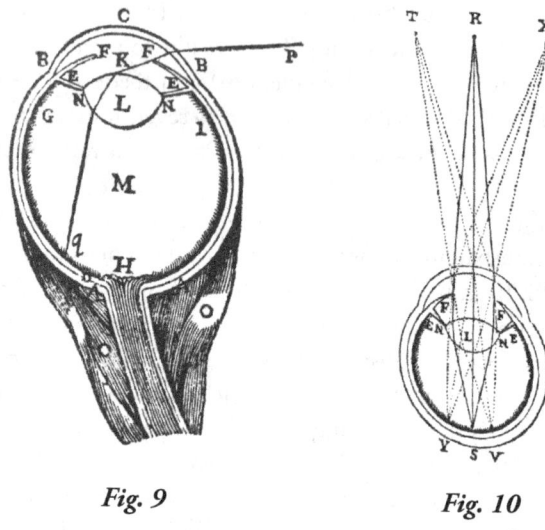

Fig. 9   *Fig. 10*

T and X, and all those in-between, would each send one its rays toward this same point S.

Now it is quite evident that the object R must act more strongly on the part of the nerve at this point S when it sends a large number of rays there than when it sends only one, and that part of nerve S must relay the action of object R to the brain more distinctly and more faithfully when it receives rays only from it alone, than if it received rays from various other objects.

The black color of the internal surface of membrane E F and of small fibers E N also helps in making vision more distinct; for, according to what was said before about the nature of this color, it deadens the force of the rays reflected from the back of the eye toward the front, thereby preventing them from returning to the back, where they might cause confusion. For example, if bodies N and F were not black, the rays of object X, on reaching point Y against the nerve, which is white, would be reflected from there in every direction toward N and F, from where they could be reflected again toward S and V, and there disturb the action of rays coming from points R and T.

The change of shape taking place in the crystalline humor enables objects at different distances to paint their images distinctly at the back of the eye. For, according to what was said in the treatise on *Dioptrics*,[9] if for example [*Fig. 11*] humor LN is of such a shape that it causes all

---

9. AT VI, 106–8.

Man 83

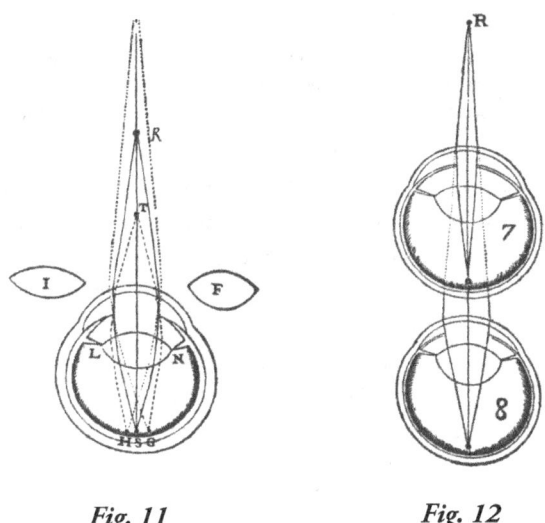

Fig. 11   Fig. 12

the rays from point R to strike the nerve precisely at point S, the same humor without its shape being changed will only cause rays from point T, which is closer, or from point X, which is farther away, to come there also; but it will cause ray T L to go toward H, and T N toward G; and on the other hand, X L will go toward G, and X N toward H, and so on for the others. Thus, in order to represent point X distinctly, the whole shape of this humor N L needs to change and become slightly flatter, like the one marked I; and to represent point T, it needs to become a little more arched, like the one marked F.

The changes in the size of the pupil serve to moderate the force of vision; for when the light is too bright, it needs to be smaller, so that too many rays do not enter the eye to damage the nerve; and it needs to be larger, when the light is weak, so that enough rays enter to be sensed. In addition, assuming the light remains constant, the pupil needs to be larger when the object viewed is distant than when it is near: for example [*Fig. 12*], if only as many rays from point R enter the pupil of eye 7 as are needed to be sensed, the same number must enter into eye 8, and consequently, its pupil must be larger.

The smallness of the pupil also serves to make vision more distinct; for you must know that whatever shape the crystalline humor may have, it is impossible for it to cause the rays coming from different points of the object to all assemble precisely at correspondingly different points. Rather, if the rays of point R, for example [*Fig. 10*], assemble precisely at point S, then only those from point T which pass through the circumference and through the center of one of the circles that can be described on the surface of this crystalline humor, can be assembled exactly at point V; and consequently, the others, which will be fewer as the pupil is smaller, will strike the nerve at other points and cannot fail to cause confusion there. As a result, if the vision of one eye is weaker at one time than at another, it will also be less distinct, whether this arises from the distance of the object or from the weakness of the light. For, the pupil being larger when the light is less strong also renders vision more confused.

From this, it also comes about that the soul will never be able to see more than a single point of the object very distinctly each time, namely, the one on which all the parts of the eye are trained at that time, other points appearing as more confused as they are farther away from it. For example, if rays from point R all assemble exactly at point S, those of point X will assemble even less exactly toward Y than those of point T will assemble toward V; and we must judge the same to be true of others, to the extent they are farther from point R. But muscles o, o turning the eye very quickly in all directions, serve to make up for this defect: for they can in no time apply it successively to all the points of the object, and thus allow the soul to see all points distinctly one after the other.

I do not add here details regarding what will give this soul the occasion to conceive all the differences in colors, since I already spoke enough about it.[10] And I also do not say which objects of vision must be agreeable or disagreeable to it; for, from what I explained about the other senses, it is easy to understand that too strong a light will injure the eyes, that moderate light will refresh them, and that among the colors, green, which consists in the most moderate action (which by analogy can be spoken of as a ratio of one to two), is like the octave among musical consonances, or like the bread among the foods we eat, that is, the one most universally pleasant. And finally, all the different fashionable colors, which are often more refreshing than green, are like the chords and passages of a new tune played by an excellent lute player, or like the dishes of a good cook that greatly stimulate the senses and make them feel more pleasure at first, but also become tedious faster than simple and ordinary objects.

---

10. See Fig. 9.

It only remains for me to say what will give the soul the means of sensing the position, shape, distance, size, and other similar qualities not relating to only one specific sense, such as those I spoke of so far, but that are common to touch and vision, and even in some respect to the other senses.

Note first that [*Fig. 13*] if hand A touches body C, for example, the parts of brain B from which the small fibers of its nerves issue will be arranged differently than if the hand touched a body of another shape, or size, or location. Thus, the soul will be able to know, by this means, the location of this body, its shape, and size, and all other similar qualities. Similarly [*Fig. 14*], if eye D is turned toward object E, the soul will be able to know the position of this object, given that

Fig. 13

the nerves from this eye will be arranged differently than if it was turned toward some other object. And it will be able to know its shape, given that rays from point 1, assembling on the nerve called optic at point 2, and those from point 3 at point 4, and so forth, will trace a shape that corresponds exactly to its own. And it will be able to know the distance from point 1, for example, given that the shape of the crystalline humor will be different than if it were closer or farther away, as was already said, to have all the rays coming from this point assemble precisely at the back of the eye at point 2, which I assume to be in the middle. Moreover, it will know the distance of point 3, and of all the others whose rays enter the eye at the same time, because the crystalline humor is so disposed that the rays of this point 3 will not assemble so exactly at point 4, as will those from point 1 at point 2, and so on with the others; and their action will be proportionately weaker, as was also said before. And finally, the soul will be able to know the size of the objects of sight, and all other similar qualities, simply through its knowledge of the distance and position of all their points, just as, reciprocally, it will sometimes judge their distance from the opinion it has of their size.

Note also [*Fig. 16*], that if the two hands *f* and *g* each hold sticks *i* and *h* with which they touch object K, then although the soul is otherwise ignorant about the length of these sticks, nevertheless, because it knows the distance between points *f* and *g* and the sizes of angles *fgh* and *gfi*, it will be able to know, as if by a natural geometry, where object K is. In the same way [*Fig. 15*], if eyes L and M are turned toward object N, the size of line L M and of angles L M N and M L N will let it know where point N is.

But it can often be quite mistaken in all this. For first, if the position of the hand or eye or finger is constrained by some external cause, it will not correspond so exactly with that of the small parts of the brain from where the nerves originate than if it depended on the muscles alone; and thus the soul, which will sense this only through the mediation of the parts of the brain, will not fail to be mistaken on such occasions.

Suppose for example [*Fig. 17*] that hand *f*, being itself disposed to turn toward o, finds itself constrained by some external force to remain turned toward K, then the parts of the brain from which its nerves originate will not be entirely arranged in the same way as they would if the hand were turned toward K by the force of the muscles. Nor will they be arranged in the same way, if the hand were really turned toward o. Rather, they are arranged in an intermediate way between these two, namely, as if the hand were turned toward P. And thus, the arrangement this constraint imposes to the parts of the brain will cause the soul to judge that object K is at point P, and that it is a different object than the one touched by hand *g*.

Similarly [*Fig. 18*], if eye M is forcibly turned away from object N, and disposed as if looking toward *q*, the soul will judge that the eye is turned toward R. And because in this situation, the rays of object N will enter the eye in the same way as would those of point S, if the eye were really turned toward R, it will believe that this object N is at point S and that it is a different object than the one being looked at by the other eye.

Similarly also [*Fig. 19*], fingers *t* and *v* touching little ball X will cause the soul to judge that they are touching two different things because they are crossed and kept forcibly in an unnatural position.

Further, if the rays—or other lines through whose mediation the actions of distant objects pass to the senses—are curved, the soul, which

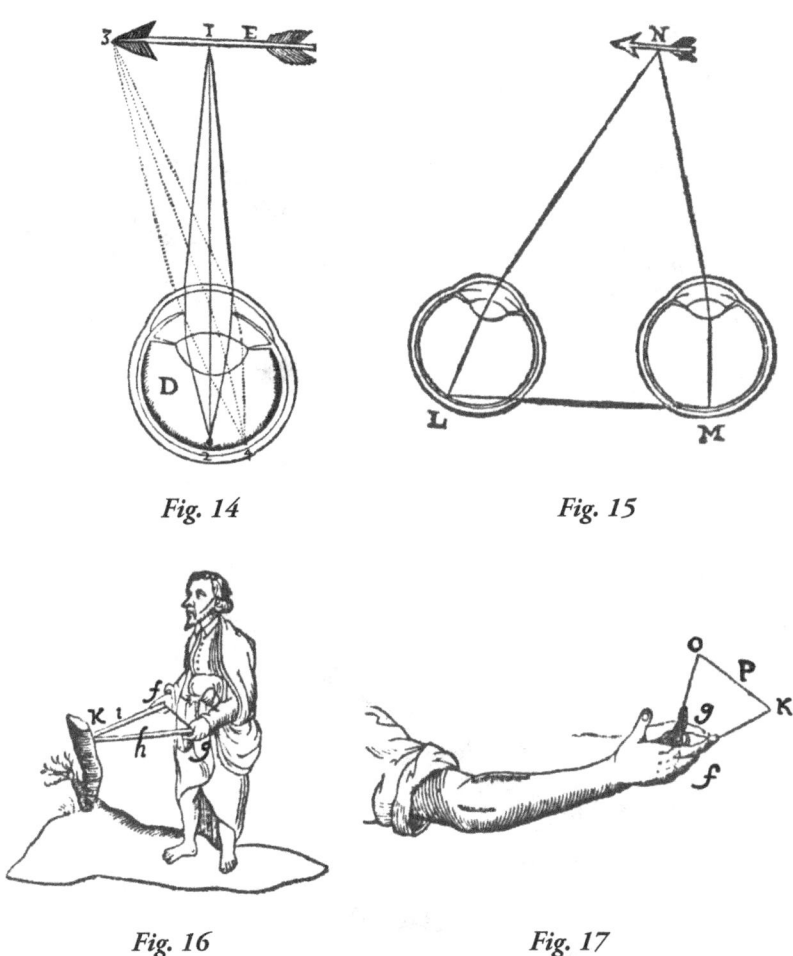

Fig. 14 *Fig. 15*

Fig. 16 *Fig. 17*

generally assumes them to be straight, will have an occasion to be mistaken. For example [*Fig. 20*], if stick HY is bent toward K, it will seem to the soul that object K, which this stick touches, is in the direction of Y. And if eye L [*Fig. 21*] receives rays from object N through lens Z that bends them, it will seem to the soul that this object is in the direction of A. And similarly [*Fig. 22*], if eye B receives rays from point D through lens c, which I assume bends them all as if they came from point E, and bends those from point F as if they came from point G, and so on with the others, it will seem to the soul that object D F H is as far away and as large as E G I appears to be.

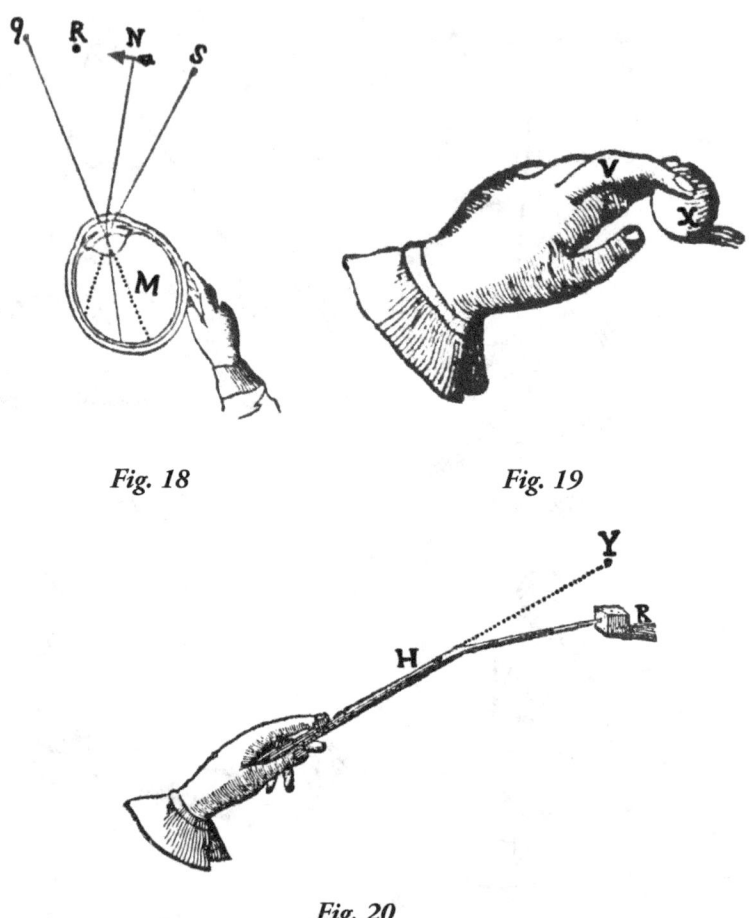

Fig. 18

Fig. 19

Fig. 20

And to conclude, it should be noted that none of the means the soul has for knowing the distance of objects of sight are certain. For [*Fig. 15*] with angles such as L M N and M L N, the change is not appreciable when the object is at fifteen or twenty feet away. As for the shape of the crystalline humor, it changes even less appreciably, for objects more than three or four feet away from the eye. And finally, as for judging distances through one's opinion of the size of the objects, or because the rays from different points of the object differ in the precision by which they assemble at the back of the eye, the example of perspectival representations shows us how easy it is to be mistaken. For, when their shapes are smaller than we imagine they should be, their colors somewhat obscure, and their outlines

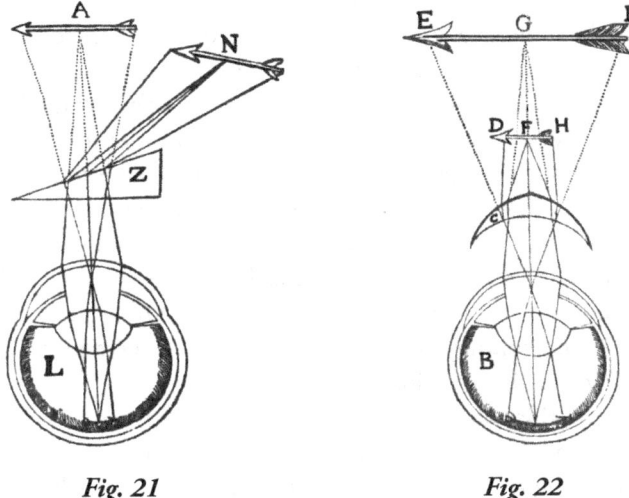

Fig. 21 *Fig. 22*

somewhat indistinct, this makes them appear to us to be much more distant and larger than they are.

Now, after having thus explained the five external senses, as they are in this machine, I must also tell you something about certain internal sensations [*sentiments*] contained in it.

Section 4. On the Internal Senses of This Machine[11]

When the liquids, as mentioned earlier,[12] serving as a sort of acid in the stomach, and entering it continuously from the whole mass of the blood through the extremities of the arteries, do not find enough food to dissolve there, so as to use up all their force, they turn it against the stomach itself and, agitating the little fibers of its nerves more strongly than usual, cause motion in the parts of the brain from which they come. This will cause the soul, being united to this machine, to conceive the general idea of *hunger*. And if these liquids are so disposed to employ their action against some specific foods rather than against others, much as ordinary acid dissolves metals more easily than wax, they will also act in a specific way on the nerves of the stomach. This will cause the soul at such times to conceive an appetite to

---

11. Again, the section titles are not by Descartes. This should probably be "On the Internal Sensations [*sentiments*] of this Machine," not "Internal Senses [*sens*]."
12. AT IX, 121.

164 eat certain foods rather than others. Now, these liquids gather mainly at the bottom of the stomach and cause the sensation of hunger there.

But many parts also rise continuously toward the throat, and when they do not come there in sufficient amount to moisten it and fill its pores in the form of water, they rise instead in the form of air or smoke, and then acting against its nerves in an unusual fashion, they cause a motion in the brain that will occasion the soul to conceive the idea of *thirst*.

165 Thus, when the blood going into the heart is purer and more subtle, and is kindled there more easily than usual, this disposes the small nerve there in the manner required to cause the sensation of *joy*; and when this blood has quite contrary qualities, it disposes the nerve in the manner required to cause the sensation of *sadness*.

And from this you can understand well enough what in this machine corresponds to all the other internal sensations in us; thus, it is time I began explaining how animal spirits run their course through the cavities and pores of its brain, and what functions depend on them.

If you have ever had the curiosity to look closely at our church organs, you know how their bellows push the air into certain receptacles—which I think are called wind-chests for this reason—and how, from there, this air enters one or another of the pipes, according to the different ways the organist moves his fingers on the keyboard. You can think of our machine's heart and arteries pushing the animal spirits into the cavities of the brain as the bellows of these organs pushing the air into the wind-chests; and the external objects making the spirits contained in these cavities enter from there into some of these pores, according to the nerves they displace, as the fingers of the organist, which, according to the keys they press, cause the air to go from the wind-chests into some pipes. The harmony of the organs does not depend on the arrangement of their pipes one sees from outside, nor on the shape of their wind-chests, or

166 other parts, but only on three things, namely, the air coming from the bellows, the pipes making the sound, and the distribution of this air in the pipes. So too, I want to point out that the functions under consideration here do not at all depend on the external shape of all those visible parts the anatomists distinguish in the substance of the brain, nor in the shape of its cavities, but solely on spirits coming from the heart, the pores of the brain they pass through, and the way those spirits are distributed in those pores. As a result, I only need here to explain in proper order what is most significant in these three things.

First, as regards animal spirits, they can be more or less abundant and their parts more or less coarse, and more or less agitated, and more or less uniform at various times; and it is by means of these four differences that all the various natural humors or inclinations in us are represented in this machine (at least insofar as they do not depend on the constitution of the brain, or on the particular affections of the soul). For, if these spirits are more abundant than usual, they are apt to stimulate motions in the machine just like those indicating in us *goodness, liberality*, and *love*; if their parts are very strong and coarse, like those indicating *confidence* or *boldness*; and if in addition, they are more uniform in shape, force, and size, *constancy*; and if they are more agitated, *promptness, diligence*, and *desire*; and if they are more uniform in their agitation, *tranquility of mind*. Whereas on the contrary, if the same qualities are lacking, these same spirits are apt to stimulate in the machine motions just like to those indicating in us *malice, timidity, inconstancy, tardiness*, and *anxiousness*.

And note that all other humors or natural inclinations depend on the ones just mentioned. Thus, the *joyous humor* is composed of promptitude and tranquility of mind; and goodness and confidence serve to make the joyous humor more perfect. The *sad humor* is composed of tardiness and anxiousness and can be augmented by malice and timidity. The *choleric humor* is composed of promptitude and anxiousness, and malice and confidence strengthen it. Finally, as I just said, liberality, goodness, and love depend upon the abundance of spirits, and form in us the humor that makes us obliging and benevolent to everyone. Curiosity and other desires depend on the agitation of their parts, and so on with the others.

But because these same humors, or at least the passions to which they dispose us, also depend very much on the impressions made in the substance of the brain, you will be able to understand them better later; and I will content myself here with relating the causes from which differences of spirits arise.

The juice of food, passing from the stomach into the veins and mixing with the blood, always communicates to it some of its qualities and, among other things, usually makes it coarser when freshly mixing with it. As a result, the small parts of this blood, which the heart sends to the brain to compose the animal spirits there, are usually not so agitated, strong, or abundant; and therefore, they do not usually make the body of this machine so light or lively, as it becomes a while after digestion is completed, and after the same blood, having passed and repassed through the heart several times, has become more subtle.

The air of respiration, also mixing in some way with the blood before it enters the left cavity of the heart, makes the blood kindle more strongly and produces more lively and restless spirits there in dry weather than in humid weather, just as we experience all kinds of flames to be more ardent at such times.

When the liver is well disposed and converts perfectly the blood going into the heart, the spirits issuing from this blood are all the more abundant and more uniformly agitated; and if the liver happens to be pressed by its nerves, the more subtle parts of the blood it contains, rising directly to the heart, will also produce more abundant and lively spirits than usual, but not so uniformly agitated.

If the gallbladder, which is intended to purge the blood of those of its parts most suited to be kindled in the heart, fails in its task, or is constricted by its nerve and the matter it contains is regorged into the veins, the spirits there will be all the more lively and more unevenly agitated.

On the other hand, if the spleen, which is intended to purge the blood of the parts least suited to be kindled in the heart, is ill-disposed, or if it is pressed by its nerves or any other body whatever, the matter it contains regorges in the veins, then the spirits will be all the less abundant and less agitated, and as a result less uniformly agitated.

In the end, whatever can cause any change in the blood can also cause one in the spirits. But above all, the little nerve terminating in the heart, being able to dilate and contract both entrances through which the blood from the veins and the air from the lungs descend, as well as the two exits through which this blood is exhaled and driven into the arteries, can cause a thousand differences in the nature of spirits—just as the heat of certain enclosed lamps the alchemists use can be moderated in many ways, depending upon whether one opens more or less the conduit through which the oil or other fuel for the flame comes in or the one through which the smoke goes out.

Section 5. The Structure of the Brain of This Machine, and How the Spirits Are Distributed There to Cause Its Motions and Sensations

Second,[13] as regards the pores of the brain, they must not be imagined other than as the gaps between the fibers of a fabric; for, in fact, the whole

---

13. In Section 4, Descartes indicated that he needed to discuss three things, "spirits coming from the heart, the pores of the brain they pass through, and the way those spirits are distributed in those pores." He then discussed the first thing and is now taking up the second.

brain is nothing other than a fabric constituted in a particular way, as I will try to explain here.

Consider its surface AA [*Fig. 23* and *24*] facing cavities EE to be like a rather thick, dense lattice or net, whose links are so many small tubes through which the animal spirits can enter, and which, always facing gland H, from where these spirits emanate, can easily turn here and there toward the different points of this gland—as you see that they are turned differently in figure 48 than in 49 [left and right sides of *Fig. 25*]. Consider that from each part of this net arise several very thin fibers, of which some are generally longer than others; after these fibers are differently interlaced through the space marked B, the longest descend toward D, then from there, comprising the marrow of the nerves, proceed to spread through all the members.

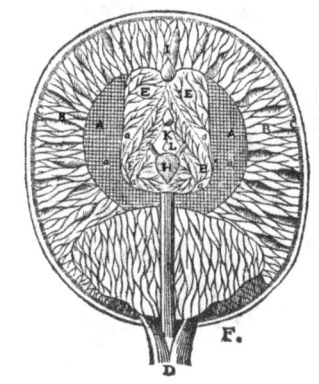

Fig. 23

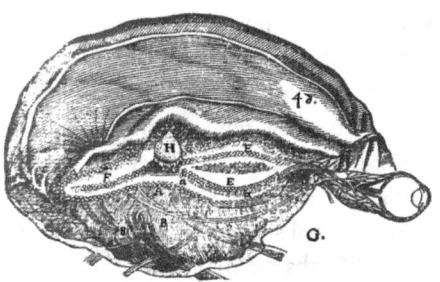

Fig. 24

Also, consider that the main qualities of these little fibers are that they can easily be bent in all kinds of ways by the sheer force of the spirits striking them and, almost as if they were made of lead or wax, that they can retain the last fold they received until they are imprinted with an opposite fold.

Finally, consider that the pores in question here are just the gaps between these fibers, and that they can be variously enlarged and constricted by the force of the spirits entering them, depending on the strength of this force and the abundance of the spirits, and that the shortest of these fibers render themselves to space *c, c* where each of them terminates at the end of one of the small vessels there and receives its nourishment from it.

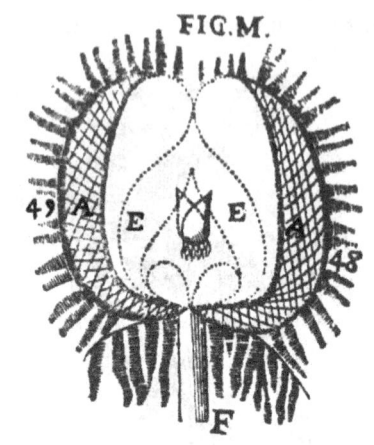

Fig. 25

Third, to explain more easily all the particularities of this fabric, I must now begin to speak about the distribution of these spirits.

The spirits never stop for a single moment in any one place; but, as they enter the cavities of brain E E [*Fig. 23* and *24*] through the holes of the little gland marked H, they tend first toward those small tubes *a, a*, which are most directly opposite them; and if tubes *a, a* are not open wide enough to receive them all, they receive at least the strongest and liveliest of their parts, while the weakest and most superfluent are pushed back toward conduits I, K, L, facing the nostrils and the palate. That is, the most agitated are pushed toward I which, if they still have much force and do not find the passage free enough, they sometimes pass out with so much violence that they tickle the inner parts of the nose, causing *sneezing*. The others are then pushed toward K and L, through which they can easily exit, because the passages there are very large; or if they fail to do so, being forced to return toward tubes *a, a* in the internal surface of the brain, they promptly cause *dizziness* or *vertigo*, which disturbs the functioning of the *imagination*.

And note, in passing, that the weaker parts of the spirits do not come so much from the arteries inserted into gland H than from those which, dividing into a thousand very thin branches, carpet the cavities of the brain. Note also that they can easily thicken into phlegm, never in the brain except in the case of some grave illness, but in those large spaces below the base of the brain, between the nostrils and the gullet, just as smoke is easily converted into soot in chimney flues, but never in the hearth where the fire is.

Also note that, when I say that the spirits leaving gland H tend toward those places of the internal surface of the brain most directly opposite to them, I do not mean that they always tend in the direction opposite them in a straight line, but only in the direction in which the disposition of the brain makes them tend.

Now, the substance of the brain being soft and pliant, its cavities would be very narrow, and almost all closed, as they appear in the brain of a dead person, if no spirit entered them; but the source producing these spirits is usually so abundant that, as they enter these cavities, they have the power to push the matter surrounding them in all directions, causing it to expand and tightening all the small nerve fibers coming from it, just as the wind, when moderately strong, can inflate the sails of a ship and tighten all the ropes to which they are attached. At such times this machine, being so arranged as to follow all the actions of the spirits, represents the body of a person who is *awake*.

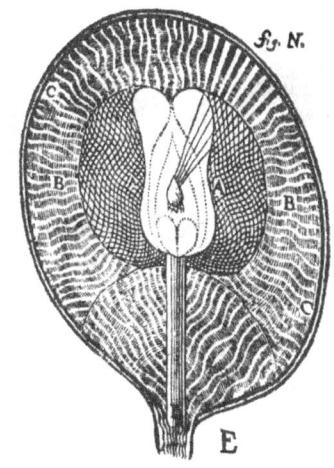

Fig. 26

Or at least the spirits have the strength to push against and stretch some parts, while the others remain free and distended, as happens with the parts of a sail when the wind is a little too weak to fill it. And at such times, this machine represents the body of a person who *sleeps*, and who has *various dreams* while sleeping. Imagine, for example, that the difference between the figures M and N [*Fig. 26, 27*, and *28*] is the same as that between the brain of a person who is awake and of a person who is sleeping and dreaming.

But, before I speak in greater detail about *sleep* and *dreams*, I must have you consider here what is most notable about the brain during the time of waking: namely, how ideas of the objects are formed in the place envisioned for the *imagination* and *common sense*, how these ideas are retained in *memory*, and how they cause the *motion of all bodily members*.

You can see, in the figure marked M [*Fig. 27*], that the spirits leaving gland H, having dilated the part of the brain marked A and partly opened all its pores, flow from there to

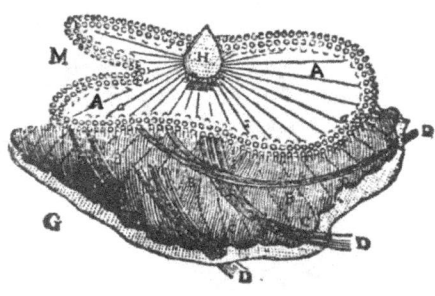

Fig. 27

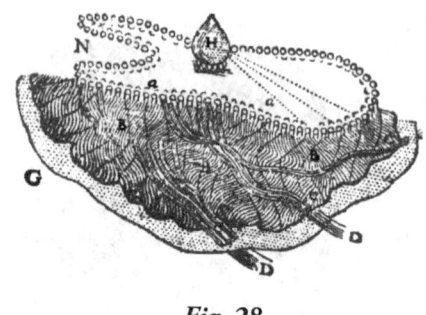

Fig. 28

B, then to C, and finally into D, from where they spread out into all the nerves. And in this way, they keep all the small fibers of which these nerves and the brain are composed so taut that even those actions that barely have enough force to move them are easily communicated from one end to the other, without the detours of the paths through which they pass preventing this.

But lest these detours keep you from seeing clearly how this is used to form ideas of objects striking the senses, note in the attached figure [*Fig. 29*] the small fibers 12, 34, 56, and the like, that make up the optic nerve and extend from the back of the eye 1, 3, 5 to the internal surface of the brain 2, 4, 6. And consider that these fibers are so arranged that, if the rays coming from point A on the object, for example, press the back of the eye at point 1, they pull the whole of fiber 12 and enlarge the opening of the small tube marked 2. Similarly, the rays coming from point B enlarge the opening of small tube 4, and so with the others. Thus, just as the different ways in which these rays exerting pressure on points 1, 3, 5 trace a figure on the back of the eye corresponding to that of object ABC, as was said before, it is evident that the different ways in which small tubes 2, 4, 6 are opened by fibers 12, 34, 56, etc., must also trace one on the internal surface of the brain.

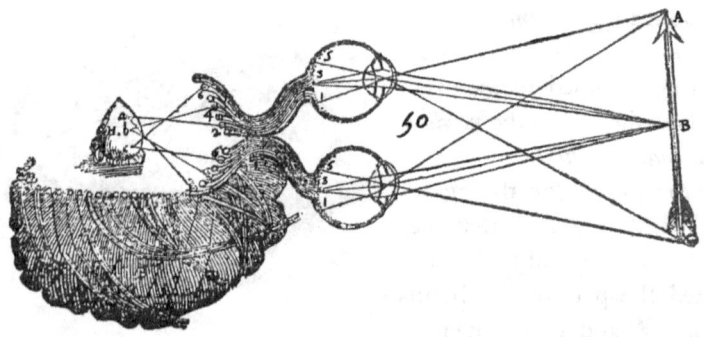

Fig. 29

Consider next that the spirits tending to enter each of the small tubes 2, 4, 6, and the like do not come indifferently from all points on the surface of gland H, but each from one specific point; those coming from point *a* of this surface, for example, tend to enter tube 2, and those from points *b* and *c* tend to enter tubes 4 and 6, and so on. As a result, at the same instant that the openings of these tubes enlarge, the spirits begin to leave the facing surfaces of the gland more freely and more rapidly than they otherwise would. And thus, just as the different ways in which tubes 2, 4, 6 are opened trace on the internal surface of the brain a figure corresponding to that of object A B C, so the different ways in which the spirits leave points *a*, *b*, *c* trace that figure on the surface of this gland.

And note that by figures, I do not mean here only the things somehow representing the position of the sides and surfaces of the objects, but also everything that, according to what I said before, can give the soul occasion to sense motion, size, distance, colors, sounds, smells, and other such qualities, and even what can make it sense titillation, pain, hunger, thirst, joy, sadness, and other such passions. For it is easy to understand that tube 2, for example, will be opened differently by the action I said causes the sensation of the color red, or titillation, than by the action I said causes the sensation of the color white, or pain; and the spirits leaving point *a* will tend differently toward this tube depending on how it is differently opened, and so for the others.

Now, among these figures, it is not those imprinted on the organs of the external senses or on the internal surface of the brain, but only those traced in spirits on the surface of gland H, *where the seat of the imagination and common sense is*, that should be taken for ideas, that is, for the forms or images the rational soul will consider directly when, united to this machine, it imagines or senses some object.

And note that I say "imagines or senses" insofar as I want to include generally under the name *idea* all the impressions that spirits can receive as they exit gland H; these are attributed to common sense when they depend on the presence of objects, but can also proceed from several other causes, as I will explain later, and should then be attributed to the imagination.

And I could add here how the traces of these ideas pass through the arteries to the heart, and thus radiate throughout the blood; and how they can sometimes even be determined by certain actions of the mother to be imprinted on the limbs of the child formed in her womb. But I will content myself with telling you more about how they are imprinted on the internal part of the brain, marked B, where the seat of *memory* is located.

Consider then, for this end, that after leaving gland H [*Fig. 29*], having received there the impression of some idea, spirits pass through tubes 2, 4, 6, and the like into pores or gaps between the small fibers of which this part B of the brain is composed. And suppose that they have the strength to widen these gaps somewhat, and to bend and arrange the small fibers they encounter, according to the different ways they are moving and the different openings of the tubes through which they pass. They do this in such a way that they also trace figures there, corresponding to those of the objects; at first, however, they do this less easily or less perfectly than on gland H, but gradually they improve as their action gets stronger and lasts longer, or is repeated more often. As a result, these figures are no longer erased so easily but are preserved in such a way that through them, the ideas previously on this gland can be formed again long afterward without requiring the presence of the objects to which they correspond. And this is what *memory* consists in.

For example, when the action of object A B C, by increasing the opening of tubes 2, 4, and 6, causes spirits to enter into them in greater quantities than they would otherwise, it also cause them, as they pass further toward N, to have the force to form certain passageways there remaining open even after the action of object A B C has ceased; or at least, if they close up again, leave a certain arrangement in the small fibers composing this part of brain N, by means of which they can be opened much more easily later than if they had not been before. This is just as if we passed several needles, or engravers' stamps, through a cloth, as you see [*Fig. 30*] in the one marked A, the small holes that would be made there would stay open, as at *a* and *b*, after the needles are withdrawn; or if they did close again, they would leave traces in the cloth, as at *c* and *d*, which would enable them to reopen very easily again.

Fig. 30

Similarly, it should be noted that, if we reopened only a few of them, like *a* and *b*, this alone could cause others, like *c* and *d*, to reopen at the same time, especially if they all had been opened several times together and had not usually been opened separately. This shows how the recollection of one thing can be excited by that of another which was imprinted in memory at the same time. For example, if I see two eyes with a nose, I immediately imagine a forehead and a mouth, and all the other parts of a face, because I am unaccustomed to seeing the ones without the others; and seeing a fire, I remember its heat, because I felt this in the past when seeing fire.

Moreover, consider that gland H is composed of very soft matter and not entirely joined and united with the substance of the brain but attached only to small arteries (whose membranes are rather loose and pliant) and kept as if in balance by the force of the blood which the heat of the heart drives toward it; thus very little force is needed to induce it to incline and lean, now more now less, now to one side now to another, and by bending down to dispose the spirits issuing from it to proceed to certain regions of the brain rather than others.

Now, there are two main causes that can make it move in this way, which I must explain here (not counting the force of the soul, which I will discuss later).

First are the differences found among the small parts of the spirits issuing from it. For if these spirits all had exactly the same force, and if there were no other cause determining the gland to lean this or that way, they would flow equally into all its pores and keep it erect and motionless at the center of the head, as is represented in figure 40 [*Fig. 31*]. But just as a body attached only by threads and kept in the air by the force of smoke coming out of a furnace would float here and there incessantly, as the different parts of the smoke acted differently against it, so also the small parts of the spirits holding up and sustaining this gland, almost always differing

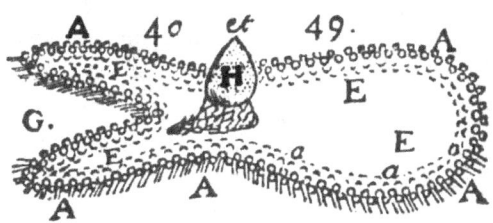

Fig. 31

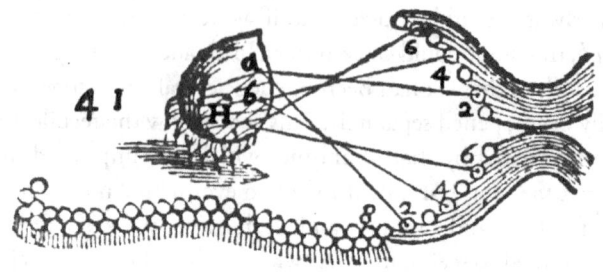

Fig. 32

in some way, must agitate it and make it lean, now to one side now to the other. As you can see in figure 41 [*Fig. 32*], not only is the center of gland H at a slight distance from the center of the brain (marked *o*), but also the ends of the arteries sustaining it are curved in such a way that almost all the spirits they bring to it proceed through region *a*, *b*, *c* of its surface toward the small tubes 2, 4, 6, and in this way opening the pores facing that direction to a greater extent than others.

Now the main effect that follows consists in that the spirits, issuing in this way from certain regions on the surface of this gland rather than from others, can have the force to turn the small tubes from the internal surface of the brain into which they flow toward the places from which they issue, unless they are already turned in that direction; and by this means, they can move

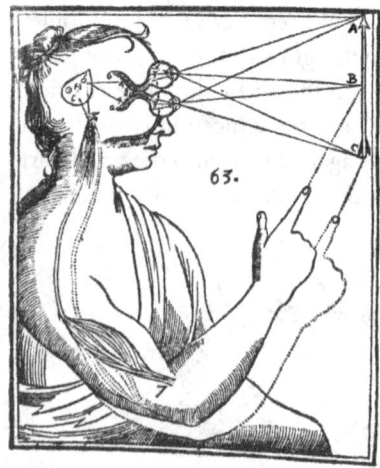

Fig. 33

the members to which these tubes correspond toward the places corresponding to those regions on the surface of gland H. And note that the idea of this motion of the members consists only in the way these spirits flow from this gland, and thus it is its idea that causes the motion.

Here [*Fig. 33*], for example, we can suppose that what makes tube 8 turn toward point *b*, rather than some other point, is only that the spirits issuing from this point tend toward it with more force than do any others. And the same thing will provide an occasion for the soul to sense that the arm is turned toward object B, if it is already in this machine, as I will later suppose it to be. For we must consider that all the points of the gland toward which tube 8 can be turned correspond to places toward which the arm marked 7 can be turned. Thus, what now makes this arm turn toward object B is that this tube is facing point *b* of the gland. But if the spirits changing their course turn this tube toward some other point of the gland, such as toward *c*, the small fibers 8 and 7 emerging around it going to the muscles of this arm, in changing their position by the same means, would close some of the pores of the brain near D and enlarge others. This would make the spirits, passing from there into these muscles in a different way than they do now, promptly turn this arm toward object C. Reciprocally, if some other action than that of the spirits entering tube 8 were to turn this same arm toward B or C, this would make tube 8 turn toward points *b* or *c* of the gland. As a result, an idea of this motion would be formed at the same time, at least if one's attention were not diverted, that is, if gland H were not prevented from leaning toward 8 by some other stronger action. And so generally, we must consider that each of the small tubes on the internal surface of the brain corresponds to a member and each of the other points of the surface of gland H to a direction toward which these members can be turned; in this way, the motions of these members and their ideas can be reciprocally caused by one another.

And moreover, to understand how, when the two eyes of this machine and the organs of the several other senses are directed toward the same object, there are not several ideas formed of it in its brain, but only one, we must consider that the spirits issuing from the same points on the surface of gland H can turn different members toward the same objects by tending toward different tubes. Thus here [*Fig. 33*], spirits issuing from the same point *b* tend toward tubes 4, 4, and 8, simultaneously turning the two eyes and the right arm toward object B.

This will be easy for you to believe if, to understand what the idea of the distance of objects consists in, you consider that, as this surface changes position, the closer a point is to the center of the brain marked *o*, the more distant are the places corresponding to them, and the farther the point is from *o*, the closer are those places. Here, for example, we should consider that, if point *b* were a little farther back than it is, it would correspond to a place more distant than B; and if it were to lean a little farther forward, it would correspond to a closer place.

Fig. 34

And when a soul is put in this machine, this will cause it to sense different objects by means of the same organs similarly arranged, without there being anything at all changing except the position of gland H. Here [*Fig. 34*], for example, the soul can sense what is at point L through the mediation of the two hands holding sticks N L and O L, because the spirits entering tubes 7 and 8 issue from point L on gland H (to which its two hands correspond). Suppose instead that gland H were a little more forward than it is, so that points *n* and *o* of its surface were at the places marked *I* and *k*, and consequently, spirits going toward 7 and 8 issue from them, the soul would sense what is at N and at O through the mediation of the same hands without their being changed in any way.

Moreover, it should be noted that when gland H is inclined in one direction by the force of the spirits alone, without the contribution of the rational soul or the external senses, the ideas formed on its surface derive not only from inequalities in the small parts of these spirits causing the corresponding difference in the humors, as was said before, but also from the impressions of memory. For if the shape of one object is imprinted much more distinctly than that of another at the place in the brain toward which this gland is inclined, the spirits issuing from it cannot fail also to receive an impression. And in this way, past things sometimes return to thought, as if by chance, and without their memory being stimulated by any object affecting the senses.

But if many different shapes are traced in this same region of the brain, each almost as perfectly as the other, as is most often the case, the spirits will receive something from the impression of each of them, and this, to a greater or lesser degree, according to the various ways their parts meet one another. This is how chimeras and hippogriffs are formed in the imagination of those who dream while awake, that is, who let their fancy wander here and there, without external objects diverting them, and without it being directed by their reason.

Fig. 35

But the effect of memory that seems to me most worthy of consideration here is that, without there being any soul present in this machine, it can naturally be disposed to imitate all the motions that real people, or many other similar machines, will perform in its presence.

The second cause that can determine the motions of gland H is the action of objects affecting the senses. For it is easy to understand [*Fig. 35*] that when the degree of opening of small tubes 2, 4, and 6, for example, is increased by the action of object A B C, the spirits beginning immediately to flow toward them more freely and more rapidly than they would otherwise, draw the gland with them a little, and cause it to incline, if it is not prevented from doing so; thus, changing the arrangement of its pores, it begins to direct a much greater quantity of spirits through *a*, *b*, and *c* to 2, 4, and 6 than it did before, which makes all the more perfect the idea that these spirits form. And this constitutes the first effect I wish you to note.

The second is that, while this gland is kept thus inclined to some side, it is prevented from easily receiving the ideas of objects acting on other sense organs. Here, for example, while almost all the spirits produced by gland H, issue from points *a*, *b*, *c*, not enough of them come from point *d* to form there the idea of object D, whose action I assume is neither as lively nor as strong as that of A B C. From this, you see how ideas impede one another, and why we cannot be very attentive to several things at the same time.

It must also be noted that the sense organs, when they are first affected more strongly by one object than others but are not yet maximally disposed to receive its action, the presence of the object suffices to dispose

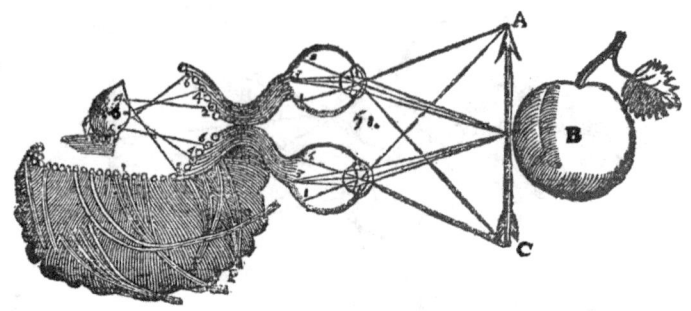

Fig. 36

them completely toward it. Thus, for example, if the eye is disposed to look at a very distant place, when a very near object ABC begins to come into view, I say that the action of this object will be able to make the eye disposed to fixate upon it at once.

And so that this may be easier to understand, consider first the difference between an eye disposed to look at a distant object, as in figure 50 [*Fig. 29*], and the same eye disposed to look at a nearer object, as in 51 [*Fig. 36*]. The difference consists not just in the crystalline humor being a little more arched and the other parts of the eye being correspondingly differently disposed in this earlier figure than in the present one, but also in that the small tubes 2, 4, and 6 being inclined toward a nearer point, and gland H being a little more advanced toward them, and in region *a*, *b*, *c* of the gland's surface being proportionately a little more arched or curved, so that in both figures, spirits issuing from point *a* always tend toward tube 2, with those from point *b*, tending toward tube 4, and from point *c* tending toward tube 6.

Consider also that the motions of gland H are themselves sufficient to change the position of these tubes, and consequently, the disposition of the eye as a whole; as was said earlier, in general, these tubes can make all the bodily members move.

Consider next that tubes 2, 4, and 6 [*Fig. 36*] can be opened by the action of object ABC, to the same extent that the eye is disposed to look at it. For, if the rays falling on point 3, for example, all come from point B, as they do when the eye looks fixedly at it, it is evident that their actions must pull more strongly on the small fibers 3, 4, than if they came in part from point A, in part from B, and in part from C, as they would if the eye were somewhat differently disposed, because then their actions, not being as similar, nor as united, cannot be as strong, often even impeding each other. This, however, occurs only when the outlines of objects are neither too similar nor too confused, as also happens with objects whose distance and parts the eye can distinguish well, as I remarked in the *Dioptrics*.[14]

Moreover, consider that gland H can be moved much more easily when inclined in the direction the eye is disposed to receive the action of whatever object acts most strongly on it, than in the opposite direction. Thus, for example, in figure 50 [*Fig. 29*], where the eye is so disposed as to look at a distant object, less force is required to make it incline slightly more forward than backward because by inclining backward, the eye would be less disposed than it was to receive the action of object A B C, which we suppose to be nearby and be the object acting most strongly on it. And this would cause the small tubes 2, 4, and 6 to be thus opened less by this action, and the spirits issuing from points *a*, *b*, and *c* would also flow less freely toward these tubes. Instead, by advancing, it would, on the contrary, make the eye better prepared to receive this action, the small tubes 2, 4, and 6 would open more, and then the spirits coming out from points *a*, *b*, and *c* would flow toward them more freely, so that, as soon as the gland would begin to move slightly thus, the course of these spirits would immediately prevail and would not allow it to stop until it was fully disposed in the way you see it in figure 51 [*Fig. 36*], and the eye would be looking fixedly at this nearby object A B C.

All that remains is to indicate what cause can thus begin to move it. Normally, it is only the force of the object itself, which, acting upon the sense organ, increases the opening of certain of the small tubes in the internal surface of the brain, so that spirits beginning promptly to flow toward them, draw this gland with them and make it incline in that direction. But in case these tubes were already as much or more open to a greater extent than this object would open them, we must consider that the small parts of the spirits flowing through its pores in every direction, being unequal, will push the gland here and there very quickly, and in the blink of an eye, without ever giving it a moment's respite. And if it happened that they should first push it in a direction toward which it is not easy for it to incline, their action, which is not very strong in itself, can hardly have any effect. On the other hand, as soon as they push it slightly in the direction in which it is already being carried, it will not fail

---

14. See *Discourse on Method*, Part VI, AT VI, 130–47.

to incline in that direction immediately, and as a result, dispose the sense organ to receive the action of its object in the most perfect way possible, as I just explained.

Let us now be done with conducting the spirits to the nerves and look at what motions depend on them. If none of the small tubes of the inner surface of the brain are not more open than any others, and consequently, the spirits have in them no impression of any particular idea, they will spread indifferently in all directions, and pass from the pores near B [*Fig. 27*], into those near C, from where the most subtle of their parts flow directly from the brain through the pores of the little membrane enveloping it, while the rest, making their way toward D, will proceed to the nerves and muscles, without causing any particular effect there, because they will be distributed to all muscles equally.

But if some tubes are more or less open, or only open in a different way than their neighbors, through the action of objects moving the senses, then the small fibers composing the substance of the brain, of which some will as a result be a little more tense or relaxed than others, will conduct the spirits toward certain regions at its base and from there to certain nerves with more or less force than to the others. This will suffice to cause different motions in the muscles, according to what was abundantly explained before.[15]

Now, I want you to conceive these motions as similar to those naturally inciting us through the various actions of the objects affecting our senses. Hence, I want you to consider six different circumstances on which they may depend. The first is the place from which the action that opens some of the small tubes through which the spirits first enter proceeds. The second consists in the force and all the other qualities of this action. The third in the arrangement of the small fibers making up the substance of the brain. The fourth in the unequal force that small parts of spirits can possess. The fifth in the different positions of the external members. And the sixth in the interplay of many actions moving the senses at the same time.

As to the place from which the action proceeds, you already know that if object A B C [*Fig. 36*], for example, acted on some other sense than vision, it would open other tubes in the internal surface of the brain than those marked 2, 4, and 6. And if it were nearer or farther away, or located elsewhere with respect to the eye than it is, it could in truth open these

---

15. AT IX, 132–38.

same tubes, but they would be located elsewhere, and therefore would be able to receive spirits from other points of the gland than from those marked *a*, *b*, and *c*, and to conduct them to regions other than A B C, where they conduct them now, and so on.

As to the various qualities of the action opening these tubes, you also know that, according to their differences, they open them differently; and we must consider that this alone is sufficient to change the course of spirits in the brain. For example, if object A B C is red, that is, if it acts on eye 1, 3, 5 in the way I said before was required to make it sense the red color, and if it has, in addition, the shape of an apple or other fruit, we must think that it will open tubes 2, 4, and 6 in a certain particular way, which will cause the parts of the brain near N to press against one another a little more than usual, so that the spirits entering through tubes 2, 4, and 6 will make their way from N through *o* toward *p*. And if this object A B C were of another color or shape, it would not be the small fibers near N and *o* that would deflect the spirits entering 2, 4, and 6 but some other neighboring ones.

And if the heat of fire A [*Fig. 37*], which is close to hand B, were only moderate, we would have to consider that the way it opened tubes 7 would cause parts of the brain near N to be pressed together and those near *o* to be spread apart a little more than usual; and thus, the spirits coming from tube 7 would go from N through *o* toward *p*. But supposing that this fire burns the hand, we must think that its action opens tubes 7 so wide that the spirits entering them have the strength to pass farther, in a straight line, than merely to N, namely, as far

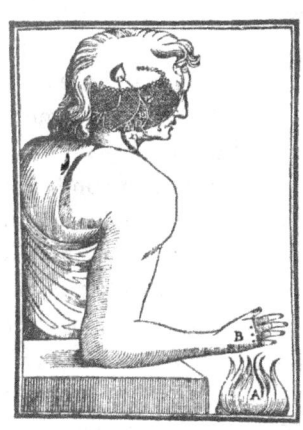

Fig. 37

as *o* and R, where, pushing before them the parts of the brain in their way, they pressure them in such a way that they are resisted and deflected toward S, and so on for the other cases.

As to the arrangement of the small fibers composing the substance of the brain, it is either acquired or natural; and since what is acquired is dependent on all the other circumstances that change the course of the spirits, I will be able to explain this better later. But to be able to tell you what the natural consists in, consider that, in forming them, God has so arranged these small fibers that the passages he left between them are able to conduct the spirits, when they are moved by a particular action, toward all of the nerves that cause the same motions in this machine that a similar action could incite in us following the instincts of our nature. Thus [*Fig. 37*], for example, if fire A burns hand B and causes the spirits entering tube 7 to tend toward *o*, these spirits find there two pores or principal passages *o*R and *os*. One of them, namely *o*R, conducts the spirits into all the nerves that serve to move the external members in the manner required to avoid the force of this action, such as in those withdrawing the hand, or arms or the entire body, and in those turning the head and eyes toward this fire to see more particularly what must be done to protect itself. And through the other passage *os*, the spirits enter all the nerves causing internal emotions, like those that occasion pain in us, such as those constricting the heart, agitating the liver, and so on. And they even enter the nerves that can cause external motions testifying to these, such as those exciting tears, wrinkling the forehead and the cheeks, and disposing the voice to cry out. Whereas, if hand B were very cold, and fire A were to warm it moderately without burning it, it would cause the same spirits entering through tube 7, no longer to proceed to O and R, but to *o* and *p*, where they would once again find pores arranged to conduct them into all the nerves that can serve for motions suited to this action.

And note that I expressly distinguished the two pores, *o*R and *os*, to alert you that two kinds of motions almost always proceed from each action, namely: external motions, serving in the pursuit of desirable things or the avoidance of harmful ones; and internal motions, commonly called *passions*, serving to dispose the heart, the liver, and all the other organs on which the temperament of the blood—and as a result that of the spirits—depends, so that the spirits produced on the occasion, cause the external motions that must follow. For, supposing that the various qualities of these spirits are one of the circumstances serving to change their course, as I will explain in a moment, one can readily think that if, for example, it is a question of avoiding some evil by force, and by overcoming or driving it away, as the passion of *anger* inclines us to do, then the spirits must be more unevenly agitated and stronger than usual. On the other hand, if the evil is to be avoided by hiding, or endured with patience, as the passion of *fear* inclines us to, then the spirits must be less abundant and weaker. For this purpose, the heart must be constricted, as if to economize the spirits and reserve them for when they are needed. And you can judge other passions correspondingly.

As for the other external motions that do not serve to avoid evil or pursue the good but just to bear witness to the passions, such as those consisting of laughter or weeping, they occur only occasionally because nerves through which spirits enter to produce them originate very close to those through which spirits enter to give rise to passions, as can be taught by anatomy.

But I have not yet shown how the various qualities of spirits can have the force to change the determination of their flow. This happens mainly when the spirits are only slightly or not at all determined. For example, if the nerves of the stomach are agitated in the way required, as I said earlier,[16] to cause the sensation of hunger, and yet nothing fit to be eaten is presented to any of the senses or to memory, then the spirits that will be caused by this action to enter tubes 8 in the brain will proceed to a region where they will find many pores disposed to conduct them indifferently into all the nerves able to serve in the search or pursuit of some object, so that only the inequality of their parts can cause them to make their way through some nerves rather than others.

And if it happens that the strongest of these parts are those tending to flow toward certain nerves, and immediately afterward toward their opposites, this will make this machine imitate the motions seen in us when we hesitate and are in doubt about something.

Similarly, if the action of fire A is intermediate between actions that can conduct the spirits toward R and p, that is, between those causing pain and those causing pleasure, it is easy to understand that the inequalities between them alone must be enough to direct them to the one or to the other, just as the same action agreeable to us when we are in a good humor can displease us when we are sad and sorrowful. And from this, you can derive the reason for all I said earlier,[17] regarding humors or inclinations, both natural and acquired, that depend on the difference in the spirits.

As for the various positions of the external members, we only need to consider that it changes the pores carrying these spirits immediately into the nerves. For example, if fire A burns hand B and the head is turned toward the left side, instead of toward the right as it is now, the spirits

---

16. AT IX, 163.
17. AT IX, 166.

would go in the same way they do now, from 7 to N, then to *o*, and from there to R and *s*. But from R, instead of going to *x*, where I assume they must pass if they are to straighten the head turned to the right, they will go to *z*, where I assume they would have to enter to straighten it if it was turned to the left. For the present position of the head, which causes the small fibers of the substance of the brain at *x* to be much more loose and easy to separate than those at *z*, when it is changed, will make, on the contrary, those at *z* to be very loose and those at *x* to be very tense and tight.

Thus, to understand how a single action can, without changing itself, move now one foot of this machine, now the other, as is required to make it walk, it suffices to consider that the spirits pass through a single pore whose extremity is differently disposed, and conducts them into different nerves when the left foot goes forward more than when the right does. And this is applicable to everything I said earlier[18] about respiration and other such motions that do not usually depend on any idea—I say usually because they may sometimes also depend on one.

Now that I think I have sufficiently explained all the functions of the waking state, and there remain only a few things to be said about *sleep*. First, we need only cast our eyes on figure 50 [*Fig. 38*], and see how the small fibers D, D going into the nerves are loose and pressed, to understand how, when this machine corresponds to the body of a sleeping person, the actions of external objects are, for the most part, prevented from reaching its brain, to be sensed; and the spirits in the brain are prevented from reaching the external members to move them. These are the two principal aspects of sleep.

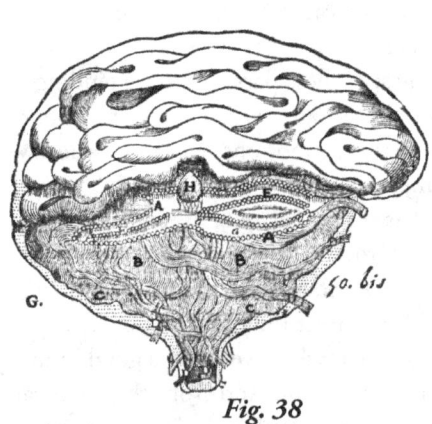

Fig. 38

As for *dreams*, they depend in part on the unequal force the spirits can have in issuing from gland H, and in part on the impressions involved in memory, so that they differ only in one way from the ideas I said

---

18. See AT IX, 138.

earlier[19] sometimes are formed in the imagination of those who dream while awake. The images formed during sleep can be much more distinct and livelier than those formed during waking. The reason for this is that the same force can open more widely the small tubes, such as 2, 4, and 6, and the pores, such as *a*, *b*, and *c*,

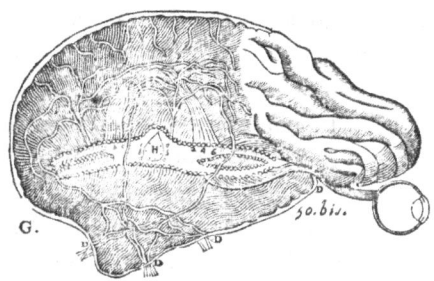

Fig. 39

serving to form these images, when the surrounding parts of the brain are loose and relaxed, as you see in figure 50 [*Fig. 39*], than when they are tense, as you can see in the earlier figures. And this also shows that if it happens that the action of some object affecting the senses should pass to the brain during sleep, it will not form the same idea that it would while awake, but will form some other more noticeable and more sensible one—as sometimes, if we are stung by a fly when asleep, we dream we are being struck with a sword, or if we are not properly covered, we imagine ourselves to be completely naked, and if we are covered too much, we think ourselves weighed down by a mountain.

Moreover, during sleep, the substance of the brain at rest has the occasion to nourish and replenish itself, being moistened by the blood contained in the little veins or arteries apparent on its external surface. Thus, after some time, its pores having become narrower, the spirits need less strength than before to keep the brain substance tense, just as the wind does not need to be as strong to inflate a ship's sails when damp than when dry. And yet these spirits are stronger to the extent the blood producing them is purified when passing several times through the heart, as noted earlier.[20] From this, it follows that this machine must naturally wake itself up after it has slept long enough, just as, reciprocally, it must also go back to sleep after it has been awake long enough, because during waking the substance of its brain is dried out, its pores being gradually enlarged by the continual action of spirits. In addition, if it happens to eat (as it does infallibly from time to time, if it can find anything to eat, because hunger

---

19. See AT IX, 174 and 184.
20. See AT IX, 168.

excites it to do so), the juice of the food mixing with its blood will render it coarser and consequently make it produce fewer spirits.

I will not stop to tell you how the machine can be prevented from sleeping by noise, pain, and other actions forcefully moving the internal parts of the brain through the mediation of the sense organs, or by joy and anger and other passions greatly agitating the spirits, the dryness of the air making the blood more subtle, or such things. Nor, on the other hand, how silence, sadness, the humidity of the air and similar things can invite sleep. Nor how a great loss of blood, too much fasting or drinking, or other such excesses that have something about them augmenting or diminishing the force of the spirits, depending on their temperaments, can make the machine wake or sleep too much. Nor how by being awake excessively, its brain can be weakened and, by excessive sleeping, grow heavy like the brain of someone senseless or stupid. Nor an infinity of other such things, insofar as they all seem to be easily deducible from what I already explained.

Now, before I move on to the description of the rational soul, I still want you to reflect a little on everything I just said about this machine, and that you consider, first, that I supposed in it only such organs or springs that can very easily persuade you wholly similar ones are both in us and in many animals lacking reason. For, as to those clearly visible by the naked eye, the anatomists already observed them all, and as for what I said about the way the arteries carry the spirits into the head, and the difference between the inner surface of the brain and its substance at its center, they will also be able to have enough visible indications to allay any doubt it, if they look a little more closely. They will not be able to doubt either these little doors or valves I placed in the nerves at the entrances to each muscle, if they take care to note that nature generally formed these valves wherever in our bodies some matter regularly enters and could tend to exit, as at the entrance to the heart, the gall bladder, the throat, the large intestines, and at the principal divisions of all the veins. Regarding the brain, they will not be able to imagine anything more likely than to say that it is composed of many small fibers variously intertwined, since all the membranes and flesh similarly appear to be composed of many filaments or fibers, and that one observes the same in all plants, so that this property seems common to all bodies able to grow and be nourished by the union and joining together of the small parts of other bodies. Finally, as to the rest of the things I assumed—things not perceivable by any sense—they are all so simple and so common, and even so few in number, that if you compare them with the diverse compositions and the marvelous ingenuity evident in the structure of the visible organs, you will have more reason to think that I omitted many that are in us, rather than having supposed some that are not. And knowing that nature always acts by the easiest and simplest means, you will perhaps judge that it is not possible to find any that are more like those nature uses than the ones proposed here.

I want you to consider next that all the functions attributed to this machine—such as the digestion of food, the beating of the heart and arteries, the nourishment and growth of bodily members, respiration, wakefulness, and sleep; the reception of light, sounds, smells, tastes, heat, and such other qualities by the external sense organs; the imprinting of their ideas on the organ of common sense and the imagination, the retention or impression of these ideas in memory; internal motions of the appetites and passions; and finally the external motions of all the bodily members, which so suitably follow the actions of the objects presenting themselves to senses and the passions and impressions involved in memory—imitate most perfectly as possible those of a real person. I want you to consider that these functions follow naturally in this machine simply from the arrangement of its organs, no more or less than the motions of a clock or other automaton follow from that of its counterweights and wheels, so that we need not on their account conceive of any soul, vegetative or sensitive, or any other principle of motion and life in it, than its blood and spirits, agitated by the heat of the fire that burns continually in its heart, and which is of no other nature than all those fires occurring in inanimate bodies.[21]

---

21. See *Discourse on Method*, AT VI, 45–46.

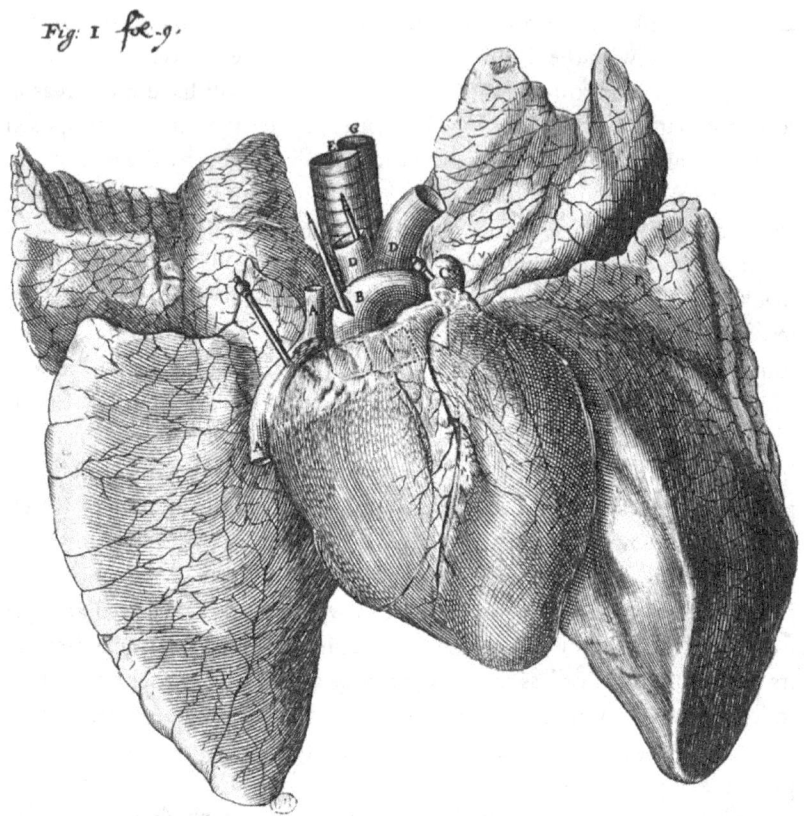

Fig. 1 of **Man *(De Homine, 1662)***
The heart and lungs with various parts labeled: A. vena cava. B. artery called arterial vein. C. vein called venal artery. D. the great artery or aorta. E. larynx. F. trachea. G. esophagus.

Appendix

A. DESCARTES ON GALILEO, 1632–1638, SELECTED

1. From Descartes to Mersenne [November–December 1632]

As for what you tell me about the calculation made by Galileo of the speed of falling bodies, it bears no relation at all to my philosophy.[1] According to my philosophy, two lead spheres, for example, one weighing a pound and the other a hundred pounds, will not have the same ratio between them as two made of wood, the one also one pound and the other a hundred— no more than two, also made of lead, one weighing two pounds and the other two hundred pounds. These are things he does not distinguish at all, which makes me believe he could not have reached the truth. But I would like to know what he writes of the ebb and flow of the sea, because it is one of the things that gave me the most difficulties to discover. Although I think I achieved this, there are however circumstances of which I am not aware.

AT I, 261

2. From Descartes to Mersenne [late November 1633]

I was at that point, when I received your last letter from the eleventh of this month, and I would like to act like the bad debtors who beg their creditors to give them a bit more time when they feel the due date of their debt approaching. In effect, I proposed to myself to send you my

AT I, 270

---

1. Referring to Galileo's *Massimi sistemi del mondo* (*Dialogue Concerning the Two Chief World Systems*, Florence, 1632), as related to him by Mersenne; "the speed of falling bodies" is calculated by Galileo in the Second Day. Galileo's theory of tides is developed in the Fourth Day.

World as a new year's gift.[2] And no more than two weeks ago, I was still resolved to send you at least a part, if all of it could not be transcribed in that time. But I tell you that in the meantime, I set myself to inquire at Leiden and Amsterdam whether Galileo's *World System* was available, because I thought I remembered that it was printed in Italy last year; I was told it was true that it was printed, but all copies of it were burned in Rome the same year, and Galileo had a fine imposed on him. This so shocked me I almost resolved myself to burn all of my papers, or at least not to let anyone see them. For I could not imagine that he, an Italian, and even well-liked by the Pope, as far as I understand, could be made a criminal for anything other than his wanting, no doubt, to establish the motion of the earth, which I know was already censored by some Cardinals. But I think I heard it was still being taught publicly afterward, even in Rome. I confess that if this view is false, all the foundations of my philosophy are as well, because it is evidently demonstrated by them. And it is so linked with all the parts of my Treatise that I would not know how to detach it without rendering the rest completely defective. But as I would never, for anything in the world, want a discourse to come from me in which even the least word disapproved of by the Church could be found, I would also much prefer to suppress it than to have it appear mutilated. I never had the temperament to publish books, and I would never have thought of bringing this one to its completion, if I had not already made promises to you and several other friends, such that the desire to keep my word obliged me much more to study. But after everything, I am sure you would not send the police after me to require my discharging my debt, and perhaps you will be happy to be exempted from the pain of reading bad things. There are already so many plausible opinions in philosophy, which can be upheld in debate, that if mine do not have anything more certain and cannot be approved of without controversy, I never want to publish them. However, because it would be bad form, if after having promised you everything for so long, I only paid you with a joke, I will not fail to show you what I did as soon as I am able; but I ask you again, please, for a year's extension to review and polish it. You drew my attention to Horace's saying: *Keep your work for nine years*,[3] and it has not been any more than three years since I

---

2. See Descartes to Mersenne (July 22, 1633), AT I, 268.
3. Horace, *Ars Poetica*, v. 388.

started the Treatise I thought to send you. I also beg you to tell me about what you know of the Galileo affair.

3. Descartes to Mersenne [February 1634]⁴

Even though I do not have anything in particular to tell you, nevertheless, because it was already more than two months that I did not hear any news from you, I believe I should not wait any longer to write you. For if I did not have overly lengthy proofs of the goodwill with which you favored me, such that I have no occasion to doubt it, I would almost fear it had gotten a bit cool, ever since I broke the promise I made you of sending something of my philosophy. But in any case, the knowledge I have of your virtue gives me hope you will not have anything but the best opinion of me, given that I wanted to suppress entirely the Treatise I wrote and lose almost all of my four years of work by giving complete obedience to the Church in its prohibition of the opinion of the earth's motion. All the same, because I did not yet see that either the Pope or the Council ratified this prohibition (it was made only by the Congregation of Cardinals established for the censure of books), I would be very happy to learn what is now held of this in France, and if their authority was sufficient to make it an article of faith. I was told that the Jesuits helped in the condemnation of Galileo. And Father Scheiner's whole book⁵ shows sufficiently that they are not among his friends. But I might add, the observations provided in his book provide so many proofs to remove the motions attributed to the sun that I could not believe that even Father Scheiner himself in his soul does not believe Copernicus's opinion; this shocks me in such a way that I do not dare write my opinion about it. As for me, I only seek rest and tranquillity of mind, which are goods that cannot be possessed by those with animosity or ambition. I will not stay, however, without anything to do, but I think for now I will teach myself; and I judge myself not very capable to be of service in instructing others, mainly those who, having already acquired some credit through false opinions, would perhaps be afraid to lose it, if the truth were discovered.

AT I, 281

282

---

4. This letter was presumably never sent but replaced by the next letter when Descartes received another letter from Mersenne in the interim.

5. Christoph Scheiner, *Rosa ursina sive Sol ex admirando facularum et macularum suarum phoenomeno varius* (Bracciano, 1626–1630).

4. Descartes to Mersenne [late February 1634]

AT I, 285

I learn from your letter that the last one I wrote to you was lost,[6] although I thought I addressed it correctly. I told you there, at length, the reason that prevented me from sending you my Treatise, a reason I do not doubt you would find so legitimate that, rather than blaming me for resolving never to show it to anyone, on the contrary, you would be the first to exhort me, had I not already fully made up my mind about this. You doubtless know that Galileo was recently reprimanded by the Inquisitors of the Faith, and his opinion concerning the motion of the earth was condemned as heretical. Now I will tell you that all the things I explained in my Treatise, which included that opinion about the motion of the earth, were so completely dependent on one another, that the knowledge one of them is false is sufficient for the recognition that all the reasons I made use of are worthless. And although I thought they were supported by very certain and very evident demonstrations, nevertheless I would not for anything in the world maintain them against the authority of the Church. I know very well it could be said that everything the Inquisitors of Rome decided is not as a result automatically an article of faith, and that it is first necessary for the Council to have accepted it. But I am not so much in love with my own thoughts as to want to make use of such exceptions, in order to have the means of maintaining them. And the desire I have to live in peace and to continue the life I embarked on, taking as my motto: *He lives well who hides well*,[7] means that I am happy to be freed from the fear I had of acquiring, by means of my writing, more knowledge than I desire, rather than angry at having lost the time and the trouble I used in composing it.

286

5. Descartes to Mersenne [around May 1, 1634]

AT I, 287

A rumor swept through here that a comet was seen recently. I beg you, if you hear anything about it, to tell it to me. And, because you wrote before that you know some people who could help me with experiments I wanted to have performed, I will tell you I read about one of them recently in *Mathematical Recreations*;[8] it consisted of a large cannon pointed straight

---

6. Probably referring to Descartes to Mersenne [late November 1633], AT I, 270–72.

7. Ovid, *Tristia* III, 4, 25.

8. Anonymous (the author appears to be the publisher Jean Appier Hanzelet), *Récreation Mathematique* (Pont-à-Mousson, 1624).

toward the zenith in the middle of a plain. I would like it if some curious people, who might have the means to do this, were to attempt it with exactness. For the author says this experiment was already done several times without the cannonball returning to earth, which might seem completely unbelievable to many people. But I do not judge it to be impossible, and I believe it is something worthy of being examined.

As for Galileo's experimental results of which you tell me, I deny them all, but I do not thereby judge that the motion of the earth is any less probable. It is not that I do not admit that the motion of a chariot, a boat, or a horse remains in some fashion in the stone after it was thrown from them; but there are other reasons preventing its remaining so great. And as for the cannonball shot from the top of a tower, it must take much longer to descend than if it were allowed to fall from the top to the base. For it meets more air on its path, which not only prevents it from moving in parallel to the horizon, but also from falling.

As for the motion of the earth, I am astonished that a man of the Church dares to write of it, however he excuses himself.[9] For I saw letters patent for the condemnation of Galileo, printed at Liege on September 20, 1633, in which are the words *although he pretended he was putting it forward only hypothetically*. Thus, they seem even to be forbidding the use of that hypothesis in astronomy. This prevents me from daring to communicate to him any of my thoughts on this subject. Moreover, since I do not yet see that this censure was authorized by the Pope or by the Council, but only by a particular congregation of Cardinal Inquisitors, I do not wholly lose hope that the same thing will happen in this case that happened with the antipodes, which were formerly condemned in pretty much the same manner,[10] and thus that, with time, my *World* will be able to see the light. But in that case, I will myself need to use my arguments.

6. Descartes to Mersenne (May 15, 1634)

I would be quite pleased to hear about Mr. Morin's account.[11] And since you saw Galileo's book, I also ask you to tell me what it contains and what

---

9. Ismael Boulliau, whose defense of Copernicanism, *Philolai, sive Dissertationis de vero systemate mundi*, was not published until 1639.

10. Condemnation of Vergilius, abbot of St. Peter's and later bishop of Salzburg by Pope Zachary in 748.

11. About longitudes, see Descartes to Mersenne [around May 1, 1634], AT I, 289.

you judged were the motives for his condemnation. I also ask you to tell me the name of the treatise you said was recently written by a churchman proving the motion of the earth—at least whether it was published. And if it was not published, I would perhaps be able to give some advice to the author that would not be useless to him.

7. Descartes to Mersenne (August 14, 1634)

I am beginning to feel the loss of not receiving news from you, and I think you were so preoccupied by the printing of the book about which you wrote to me, that this took up all of your free time.[12] Mr Beeckman came here Saturday night and loaned me Galileo's book,[13] but he took it back to Dordrecht this morning, so I had it in my hands for only thirty hours. I was able to flip through the whole book; and I find he philosophizes well enough about motion, even though he has very little to say about it I find entirely true. But as for what I can see, he is more deficient when he follows received opinions than when he deviates from them, except, however, when he discusses the ebb and flow of the tides, which I find to be a bit far-fetched. I also explained this by the motion of the earth in my *World*, but in a way completely different than his. However, I would like to admit I found several of my own thoughts in his book, as among others two I believe I already wrote to you about. The first is that the spaces heavy bodies pass through as they fall are as to the squares of the time of descent. That is, if a ball uses three moments to fall from A to B, it will only require one to continue from B to C, etc. This is what I said, with many qualifications, as in fact it is not entirely true, as he thinks he demonstrated. The second is that the turns and returns of the same string are all made in almost the same amount of time, even though one can be much larger than another.

His arguments to prove the motion of the earth are very good. But it seems to me that he does not present them as he should to make them

---

12. In 1634 Mersenne published five works, all with Paris publishers. The printing of two of them, *Questions inouyes ou Récréation des sçavans* and *Questions harmoniques*, ended in December 1633. Setting aside *Les mécaniques de Galilée*, Descartes might then be referring to *Les préludes de l'harmonie universelle* or *Questions théologiques, physiques, morales et mathématiques*.

13. Galileo, *Massimi sistemi del mondo* (*Dialogue Concerning the Two Chief World Systems*, 1632).

persuasive, as the digressions he mixes in between are the reason the first arguments are not remembered when the last ones are read.

As for what he says about a cannon fired parallel to the horizon, I believe you will find there some sufficiently noticeable differences, if you were to perform the experiment precisely.

As for the other things you write to me about, the messenger does not allow me enough time to respond to them. Also, it would be impossible for me to absolutely resolve any question of physics without first having explained all of my principles, something impossible except through the Treatise I am resolved to suppress.

The words from the Liège publication are: *Thus, the aforementioned Galileo was summoned to the Sacred Tribunal of the Inquisition, interrogated and detained in prison, and confessed in a previous interrogation. He showed himself again to be firmly of the same opinion, even though he pretended to say it was proposed only as a hypothesis. As a result, the matter having been thoroughly deliberated, the Most Eminent Cardinals, General Inquisitors, acting as a Tribunal, pronounced and declared that the aforementioned Galileo seemed strongly suspect of heresy, insofar as he became a follower of a false doctrine which is contrary to Holy and Divine Scriptures—namely, that the sun is at the center of the world and does not move from sunrise to sunset, whereas the earth does move and is not the center of the world—or he has been of the opinion that this doctrine could be defended as probable, even though it was declared contrary to the Sacred Scriptures, etc.*

8. From Descartes to [Mersenne] [March 1635]

As for the telescopes, I would tell you that since the condemnation of Galileo, I revised and completely finished the Treatise I started earlier. Having entirely separated it from my *World*, I intend to print it by itself in a short while. However, because more than a year might have to pass before anyone can see it in print, if Mr N.[14] wants to work on it before that time, I would take him up on the favor and offer to copy everything I put in it regarding practice, and to send it to him whenever it pleases him. [. . .]

As for heat, I do not believe it is the same thing as light or rarefaction of air. Instead, I conceive it as a completely different thing, which can often arise from light, and from which rarefaction can result. I also do not

---

14. Possibly the mathematician and Descartes's correspondent Florimond Debeaune.

believe, as the philosophers imagine, that heavy bodies fall by some *real quality* named *heaviness*, nor also by some attraction to the earth. But I will not be able to explain my opinion of all these things without presenting my *World* with the proscribed motion, something I now judge to be out of season. I am surprised that you propose to refute the book *Against the Motion of the Earth*,[15] but I leave it to your discretion.

9. From Descartes to Mersenne [March 1, 1638]

AT II, 24, 26

As for the one who you say accuses me of not citing Galileo, he demonstrates a wish to reprimand and does not have a ground to do so, for Galileo himself does not attribute to himself the invention of telescopes, and I did not need to speak of anyone but the inventor.[16] I did not need to cite those who wrote before me about optics either, for my intent was not to write a history, and I contented myself in saying, in general, there were people who already discovered many things, so that it could not be imagined that I wanted to attribute to myself the inventions of others. In this I did more wrong to myself than to those who I forgot to cite, for one can think that they did much more than one can perhaps find by reading them, if I had indicated who they are.

10. From Descartes to Mersenne [June 29, 1638]

AT II, 174

Your last letter only contains some observations on Galileo's book,[17] to which I do not know how to respond, because I did not yet see it. As soon as it will be for sale, I will look at it, if only to be able to send you my annotated copy, if it is worth the trouble, or at least to send you my observations of it.

11. From Descartes to Mersenne (July 27, 1638)

AT II, 254

[. . .] I did not yet see Galileo's book,[18] even though I sent word to Leiden to have it sent to me.

---

15. Likely Jean-Baptiste Morin, *Responsio pro Telluris quiete ad Jacobi Lansbergii Apologiam pro Telluris motu* (Paris, 1634).

16. See AT VI, 82.

17. Galileo, *Two New Sciences* (*Discorsi e dimostrazioni matematiche intorno a due nuove scienze*) (Leiden, 1638).

18. See Descartes to Mersenne [June 29, 1638], AT II, 194.

12. From Descartes to Mersenne [October 11, 1638]

I will begin this letter with my observations on Galileo's book.[19] I find, in general, that he philosophizes much better than is common, insofar as he abandons the errors of the Schools as much as he can and attempts to examine matters in physics by mathematical reasons. In this, I agree entirely with him, and I hold there is no other means to discover the truth. But it seems to me that he lacks a great deal in that he continually digresses and does not stop to explain any subject fully. This shows he did not examine them in an orderly way, and that, without considering the first causes of nature, he looked only for the causes of some particular effects and thus he built without a foundation. Now, the closer his manner of philosophy is to the truth, the more easily we can see its faults, in the same way, we can better say when those who sometime follow the correct path go astray, than when those who never follow it do.[20]

AT II, 380

---

19. Galileo, *Two New Sciences* (*Discorsi e dimostrazioni matematiche intorno a due nuove scienze*) (Leiden, 1638).

20. Descartes continues this letter with his "Notes on Galileo," that is, his reading notes on Galileo's *Two New Sciences*. There are further mentions or discussion of Galileo's *Two New Sciences* in Descartes to Mersenne (November 15, 1638), AT II, 420–40; Descartes to Mersenne [early December 1638], AT II, 462; Descartes to Mersenne (February 9, 1639), AT II, 495–96; Descartes to [Debeaune] (February 20, 1639), AT II, 510; Descartes to Mersenne [February 20, 1639], AT II, 523; Descartes to Mersenne (December 25, 1639), AT II, 630–31; and Descartes to Mersenne (January 29, 1640), AT III, 9–11. Descartes to Mersenne (June 11, 1640), AT III, 72, has the following interesting statement: "You write to me of Galileo as if he was still living, and I thought he died a long time ago. Whether it is true that he had exact tables for the aspects and eclipses of the planets of Jupiter, it is certain he did more than anyone concerning longitudes; but I am surprised he could have made such tables, seeing that we still have not been able to make them for the moon. [. . .] The way I explain the ebb and flow of the sea has nothing at all in common with that of Galileo." Further references to Galileo can be found in Descartes to Mersenne (September 15, 1640), AT III, 175; Descartes to Mersenne (March 31, 1641), AT III, 349–50; Descartes to Huygens (October 10, 1642), AT III, 796–98; Descartes to Huygens (February 18, 1643), AT III, 811–12; Descartes to Mersenne (February 23, 1643), AT III, 633; Descartes to Colvius (April 20, 1643), AT III, 646; Descartes to Unknown [1641–1644], AT V, 544–45; Descartes to Dupuy (January 5, 1645), AT IV, 150–51; and Descartes to Mersenne [September 1647], AT V, 74–77.

B. DESCARTES, *DISCOURSE ON METHOD*, PART V

I would be very happy to continue, and to show here the whole chain of other truths I deduced from these first ones.[21] But because I would need to speak about many questions that are matters of controversy among the learned, with whom I do not wish to quarrel, I believe it will be better for me to abstain from this and only say in general what these questions are, to let wiser people judge whether it would be useful for the public to be more specifically informed about them. I have always remained firm in the resolution I made not to assume any principle than the one I just used to demonstrate the existence of God and of the soul, and not to accept anything as true that did not seem to me clearer and more certain than did the demonstrations of the geometers; and nevertheless, I dare to say, not only did I find a way to satisfy myself within a short time regarding all the principal difficulties we are accustomed to dealing with in philosophy, but also I noticed certain laws that God has so established in nature, and of which he has imprinted in our souls such notions that, after having reflected sufficiently on them we cannot doubt that they are strictly observed in everything existing or occurring in the world. Then, in considering what follows from these laws, it seems to me I discovered many truths more useful and more important than anything I previously learned or even hoped to learn.

I tried to explain the principal ones of these truths in a treatise which certain considerations prevent me from publishing.[22] But I do not know of any way to make them better known than by summarizing here what the treatise contains. Before I started to write the treatise, my aim was to include in it everything I thought I knew regarding the nature of material things. But, just as painters, unable to represent all the different sides of a solid body equally well on a flat surface choose one of the principal sides that they bring to light and shade the others, make them appear only as they can be seen from the perspective of the chosen side, so also, fearing I would not be able to put into my discourse everything I had

---

21. Referring to the metaphysical principles described in *Discourse on Method*, Part IV, about the existence of God and the nature of our souls, and the foundations of the physics he claimed to deduce from them.

22. A reference to the treatise of which *Le Monde or Treatise on Light* and *Man* are part.

in mind, I undertook merely to expound fully what I conceived about light; then, using that occasion, to add something about the sun and the fixed stars, because light proceeds almost entirely from them; something about the heavens, because they transmit it; about planets, comets, and the earth, because they reflect it; about all terrestrial bodies in particular, because they are either colored, or transparent, or luminous; and finally about man, because he is the observer of these things. Moreover, to cast a little shadow on all these things, and to be able to say more freely what I judged about them, without being obliged to follow or refute the opinions accepted among the learned, I resolved to leave everyone here to their disputes. I decided to speak only of what would happen in a new world, if God had now created somewhere, in imaginary spaces, enough matter to compose it, and agitated the different parts of this matter in various ways and without order, so that he composed from it a chaos as confused as the poets could invent, and that afterward he did nothing other than lend his ordinary concurrence to nature, and let it act in accordance with the laws he established. Thus, first, I described this matter and tried to represent it so that there is nothing in the world, it seems to me, clearer or more intelligible, except what was just said about God and the soul; for I even explicitly supposed that there was in this matter none of those forms or qualities disputed in the Schools, nor generally anything the knowledge of which was not so natural to our souls that we could not even pretend to be ignorant of it. Moreover, I showed what the laws of nature were; and, without basing my reasons on any other principle but the infinite perfections of God, I tried to demonstrate all those laws about which we could have any doubt, and to show that they are such that even if God created several worlds, there could not be any in which they failed to be observed. After that, I showed how, because of these laws, the greater part of the matter of this chaos was disposed and arranged in a certain way, which made it similar to our heavens; how, at the same time, some of its parts composed an earth and others some planets and comets, and still others a sun and fixed stars. And here, expanding on the subject of light, I explained at length what was this light present in the sun and the stars, and how from there it traveled in an instant across the immense spaces of the heavens, and how it was reflected from the planets and comets to the earth. I also added several things concerning the substance, situation, motions, and all the various qualities of these heavens and stars; in this way I thought I said enough to show that nothing observed in the heavens

43

and stars of this world should not, or at least could not, appear quite like in those of the world I was describing. From there I went on to speak in particular about the earth: how, although I expressly supposed that God put no weight in the matter of which it was composed, none of its parts failed to tend precisely toward its center; how, there being water and air on its surface, the arrangement of the heavens and the stars, mainly of the moon, has to cause there an ebb and flow similar in all respect to what we observe in our seas, as well as a certain current of both water and air, from east to west, such as we also observe between the tropics; how mountains, seas, springs, and rivers could be formed there naturally, and metals could be found in mines, and plants grow in the fields, and generally how all the bodies called mixed or composite could be engendered there. And, among other things, because other than the stars I know of nothing else in the world except fire that produces light, I tried to make everything belonging to its nature clearly understood: how it is made, how it is nourished, how it sometimes has heat without light, and sometimes light without heat; how it can introduce various colors and various other qualities into various bodies; how it melts some and hardens others; how it can consume almost all of them or convert them into ashes and smoke; and finally how from these ashes, by the sheer force of its action, it produces glass—I took particular pleasure in describing this transmutation of ashes into glass because it seemed to me to be as admirable as any taking place in nature.

Yet I did not want to infer from all these things that this world was created in the way I proposed, for it is much more likely that from the beginning God made it just as it had to be. But it is certain, and this is an opinion commonly accepted among theologians, that the action by which God now preserves it is precisely the same as that by which he created it. So, even if in the beginning he had never given it any other form than that of chaos, provided that he established the laws of nature and lent nature his concurrence to act as it normally does, we can believe, without doing injustice to the miracle of creation, that by this means alone all things purely material could over time have come to be just as we see them now. And their nature is much easier to conceive, when we see them coming to be little by little in this manner, than when we consider them only in their completed state.

From the description of inanimate bodies and plants, I passed to that of animals and, in particular, to that of men. But I did not yet have sufficient knowledge to speak of them in the same manner as I did the rest, that is, by demonstrating effects from causes and showing what seeds and in what manner nature must produce them. Thus, I contented myself with supposing that God formed the body of a man exactly like one of ours, as much in the external shape of its members as in the internal arrangement of its organs, composing it only out of the matter I had described and at the beginning without putting into it any rational soul, or anything else to serve as a vegetative or sensitive soul, but rather that he kindled in its heart one of these fires without light I had already explained, and whose nature I conceived to be no other than what heats hay when it is stored before it is dry, or that causes new wines to boil when they are left to ferment on crushed grape residues. For, on examining the functions that could as a result be in this body, I found there precisely all those that may occur in us without our thinking about them, and hence without our soul contributing to them, that is, from that part of us, distinct from the body, of which it was said previously that its nature is only to think. And these functions are just the ones in which animals without reason may be said to resemble us. But I could find none of the functions there which, being dependent on thought, are the only ones that belong to us as men; instead, I found these all there afterward, once I supposed that God created a rational soul and joined it to this body in a particular way I described.

But so that you can see how I treated this matter, I want to give here the explanation of the motion of the heart and the arteries; for, being the first and the most general motion we observe in animals, it will enable us to judge easily what we should think of all the others. And so that it will be less difficult to understand what I will say about it, I would like people who are not at all versed in anatomy to take the trouble, before reading this, to have dissected in front of them the heart of some large animal with lungs, because such a heart is in all respects quite similar to that of man, and to have the two chambers or cavities in it shown to them. First, there is a cavity on the right side of the heart, into which two very large tubes are connected, namely, the vena cava, which is the main receptacle of the blood and like the trunk of a tree of which all other veins in the body are the branches, and the arterial vein (which was thus misnamed, because it is indeed an artery), which, originates in the heart and after leaving it divides into many branches spreading throughout the lungs. Then there is the cavity on the left side, likewise connected to two tubes as large or much larger than the previous ones, namely, the venous artery (which has also been misnamed since it is nothing but a vein), which comes from the lungs, where it is divided into many branches intertwined with those of the arterial vein and which those of the conduit called the windpipe, through which the air we breathe enters, and the great artery which, issuing from the heart, sends its branches throughout the body. I would also like people to be shown the eleven little membranes which, like so many little doors, open and close the four openings in these two cavities: namely, three at the entrance to the vena cava, where they are so arranged that they cannot in any way prevent the blood it contains from flowing into the right cavity of the heart, and yet effectively prevent it from flowing out; three at the entrance to the arterial vein, which, being arranged in the opposite way, allow the blood in this cavity to pass into the lungs, but do not allow the blood in the lungs to return there; likewise, two others at the entrance to the venous artery, which let the blood flow from the lungs to the left cavity of the heart but prevent its return; and three at the entrance to the great artery, which allow the blood to leave the heart, but prevent it from returning there. There is no need to look for any other reason for the number of these membranes, except that the opening of the venous artery, being oval, because of its location, can be conveniently closed with two, while the other openings, being round, can better be closed with three. Further, I would like people to consider that the great artery and the arterial vein are of a much harder and firmer composition than are the venous artery and the vena cava; that the latter two enlarge before entering the heart and form there two pouches, called the auricles, which are composed of a flesh similar to that of the heart; that there is always more heat in the heart than anywhere else in the body; and finally that this heat is capable of causing a drop of blood to swell and quickly expand as soon as it enters its cavities, just as liquids generally do when they fall drop by drop into some very hot vessel.

After that, I need to say a little to explain the motion of the heart. When its cavities are not full of blood, blood necessarily flows from the vena cava to the right cavity and from the venous artery into the left cavity, since these two vessels are always full of blood, and their openings, which face the heart, cannot then be blocked. But as soon as two drops of blood have entered in this way, one in each of its cavities, these drops, which must be very large since the openings through which they enter are very wide, and the vessels from which they come are very full of blood, become rarefied and dilate, because of the heat they find there. In this way, they cause the whole heart to swell, and they push against and close the five small doors at the entrances of the two vessels from which they come, thus preventing more blood from descending into the heart; and, continuing to become more and more rarefied, they push open the six other little doors at the entrance to the other two vessels, through which they exit, causing all the branches of the arterial vein and of the great artery to swell at almost the same instant as the heart. Immediately after the heart deflates, as do these arteries as well, because the blood that entered it cools down and the six little doors close, while the five doors of the vena cava and the venous artery reopen and allow passage to two more drops of blood, which once again swell the heart and the arteries, exactly as before. And because the blood thus entering the heart passes through these two pouches, which are called the auricles, it follows that their motion is contrary to its own, and they become deflated when the heart is inflated. Now, so that those who do not know the force of mathematical demonstrations and are not accustomed to distinguishing true reasons from probable ones, do not venture to deny this without examining it, I want to caution them that this motion I just explained also necessarily follows just from the arrangement of the parts of the heart that can be seen with the naked eye, and from the heat that can be felt with the fingers, and from the nature of the blood that can be known by experience—just as the motion of a clock follows from the force, position, and shape of its counterweights and its wheels.

But you may ask why the blood of the veins is not dissipated when flowing continuously into the heart, and why the arteries are not overly full of blood, since all the blood passing through the heart flows through them. I do not need to answer this other than what was already written by an English physician, who must be praised for having broken the ice on this subject.[23] He is the first who taught that there are many small passages at the extremities of the arteries through which the blood they receive from the heart enters the small branches of the veins, from there going again to the heart, so that its course is nothing but a perpetual circulation. He proves this very well from the common experience of surgeons, who, binding an arm moderately tightly, above a vein they opened, cause the blood to flow out more abundantly than if they had not bound it. And the opposite would happen if they bound the arm

---

23. William Harvey (1578–1657), author of *De motu cordis* [...] (*Anatomical Account of the Motion of the Heart and Blood*, 1628).

below, between the hand and the opening, or if they bound it very tightly above the opening. For it is obvious that a somewhat tight binding can prevent the blood already in the arm from returning to the heart through the veins but does not prevent blood from coming in through the arteries because they are located below the veins, and their membranes, being harder, are less easy to press; and also because the blood coming from the heart tends to pass through the arteries toward the hand with more force, than it does in returning from there toward the heart through the veins. And since this blood leaves the arm through the opening in one of the veins, there must necessarily be some passages below the binding, that is, toward the extremities of the arm, through which it could come from the arteries. He also proves very well what he says about the circulation of the blood by referring to some small membranes so arranged in various places along the veins that they do not allow the blood to pass from the middle of the body toward the extremities, but only to return from the extremities toward the heart. He further proves this by an experiment showing that all the blood in the body can flow out of it in a very short time through a single cut artery, even if the artery is tightly bound close to the heart and cut between it and the binding, so that no one could have reason to imagine that the blood flowing out came from elsewhere than the heart.

But there are many other things showing that the real cause of this motion of the blood is what I stated. First, the difference one notices between blood leaving the veins and blood leaving the arteries can only result from the fact that it is rarefied and, as it were, distilled when passing through the heart; it is subtler, livelier, and warmer immediately after leaving it, that is, when in the arteries, than it is shortly before entering them, that is, when in the veins. And if we look carefully, we will find that this difference is more evident near the heart than in places farther from it. Then, the hardness of the membranes of which the arterial vein and the great artery are composed shows well enough that the blood beats against them with more force than against the veins. And why would the left cavity of the heart and the great artery be larger and wider than the right cavity and the arterial vein, unless the blood from the venous artery, having been only in the lungs after passing through the heart, is subtler and more easily rarefied stronger than the blood coming immediately from the vena cava? And what can physicians conclude from taking the pulse, if they do not know that, as the nature of the blood changes, it can be rarefied by the heat of the heart, more or less strongly, and more or less quickly than before? And if we examine how this heat is communicated to the other members, must we not admit that it is by means of the blood, which, passing through the heart, is reheated there, and from there spreads through the whole body? Thus, if we remove the blood from some part of the body, by the same means, we remove the heat from it; and even if the heart were as hot as a glowing iron, it would not be enough to reheat the feet and the hands as it does, unless it continually sent new blood to them. Then, too, we know from this that the real use of respiration is to bring enough fresh air into the lungs to cause the blood coming there from the right cavity of the heart, where it was rarefied and, as it were, changed into vapors, again thickens there, and converts into blood, before returning to the left cavity; without this, the blood would not be suitable as nourishment for the fire there. This is confirmed because we see that animals without lungs have only one cavity in the heart, and that children who cannot use their lungs while enclosed within their mother's womb, have an opening through which blood flows from the vena cava into the left cavity of the heart, and a tube through which the blood goes from the arterial vein into the great artery, without passing through the lung. Then how would digestion take place in the stomach, if the heart did not send heat there through the arteries, together with some of the most fluid parts of the blood, which help to dissolve the food that went there? And is it not easy to understand the action converting the juice of this food into blood, if we consider that, passing and repassing through the heart, it is distilled perhaps more than one hundred or two hundred times a day? And what more is needed to explain nutrition and the production of the various humors in the body? We need only say that the force with which the blood, in being rarefied, passes from the heart toward the extremities of the arteries, is such that some of its parts stop in parts of the body where they drive out and take the place of other parts of the blood, and that, according to the situation or shape or size of the pores they encounter, some of them go to certain places rather than others, in just the same way that anyone can have seen various sieves with holes of different sizes, serve to separate different grains from each other? And finally, what is most remarkable in all of this is the generation of animal spirits, which are like a very subtle wind, or rather like a very pure and lively flame, which rises continuously in great abundance from the heart to the brain, and from there goes through the nerves into the muscles and gives motion to all the members. The most agitated and penetrating parts of the blood, and thus the best suited to compose these spirits, go to the brain rather than elsewhere. There is no need to imagine any other cause for this than that the arteries carrying these parts of the blood there are those coming from the heart most in the straightest line of all, and that, according to the rules of mechanics, which are the same as those of nature, when many things tend to move together toward a place where there is not enough room for all of them, as when the parts of blood coming from the left cavity of the heart all tend toward the brain, the weakest and least agitated ones must be pushed aside by the strongest ones, which, by this means, arrive there alone.

I explained all these things in great detail in the treatise I previously intended to publish. And then I showed there what structure the nerves and muscles of the human body must have to make animal spirits inside them with the strength to move its members, as we see when heads, shortly after being severed, still move and bite the earth although they are no longer alive. I also showed what changes must occur in the brain to cause waking, sleep, and dreams; how light, sounds, smells, tastes, heat, and all other qualities of the external objects can imprint various ideas on the brain through the mediation of the senses; how hunger, thirst, and other internal passions can also send their ideas there. And I showed what part of them must be taken there for the common sense where these ideas are received, memory, which preserves them, and imagination, which can change them in various ways and compose new ideas; and, by distributing animal spirits to the muscles, it can move the members of this body in as many different ways and in a manner appropriate to the objects presented to its senses and the internal passions in the body, as our body can without being guided by the will. This will not seem at all strange to those who know how many different *automatons* or moving machines human ingenuity can make, using very few parts compared to the great multitude of bones, muscles, nerves, arteries, veins, and all the other parts in the body of every animal. For they will regard this body as a machine which, having been made by the hands of God, is incomparably better ordered, and contains in itself more admirable motions, than any of those that can be devised by people.

And here I specifically paused to show that, if there were such machines having organs and the outward form a monkey or some other animal that lacked reason, we would have no way of recognizing that they were not entirely of the same nature as these animals; whereas if there were any such machines with a resemblance to our bodies and imitating our actions as much as it would be morally possible,[24] we would still have two very certain means to recognize that they would not for those reasons be real humans. The first is that they could never use words or other signs, composing them as we do, to declare our thoughts to others. For we can easily conceive a machine made in such a way that it utters words, and even utters words appropriate to corporeal actions causing some change in its organs (such as, if it is touched in a certain place, it asks what we want to say to it, or, if in another, it cries out that we are hurting it, and the like). But it does not arrange words differently to answer the sense of everything that will be said in its presence, as the stupidest people can do. And the second is that, although they might do many things as well or perhaps better than any of us, they would inevitably fail in some others, by which we would discover that they would not be acting through knowledge, but solely through the disposition of their organs; for, while reason is a universal instrument that can serve in all kinds of occasions, these organs need a particular disposition for each particular action; hence it is morally impossible for there to be enough diversity in a machine to make it act in all occurrences of life in the same way our reason makes us act.

Now, by these two same means, we can also know the difference between humans and animals. For it is a very remarkable thing that there are no humans so dull and stupid, without even excluding the insane, that they are not capable of arranging together various words and composing a discourse by which they make their thoughts understood; and, on the other hand, there is no other animal, as perfect and as well-formed as it may be, that does the same. This does not happen because they lack the organs, for we see that magpies and parrots can utter words just as we can, and yet cannot speak as we do, that is, by showing that they are thinking what they are saying; in contrast, people born deaf and dumb are deprived, as much or more than animals, of the organs others use to speak, yet they are accustomed to invent some signs for themselves,

---

24. Descartes qualifies something as "morally" possible, impossible, or certain when it fails to be absolutely so. In *Principles of Philosophy* IV, article 205, he says that moral certainty is "a certainty that suffices for the conduct of life, though if we regard the absolute power of God, what is morally certain may be uncertain."

by which they make themselves understood by those who are regularly with them and have the time to learn their language. And this shows not merely that animals have less reason than humans, but that they have none at all; for we see that very little is required to know how to speak. And this is more so since we observe inequality between animals of the same species, in the same way as we do between humans, some being easier to train than others; it is not credible that a monkey or a parrot, which would be the most perfect of its species, would not equal in this respect a stupid child, or at least a child with a disordered brain, if their souls were not of a nature entirely different from ours. And we must not confuse words with the natural motions that show passions and can be imitated by machines as well as animals. Nor should we think, like some of the ancients, that animals speak, although we do not understand their language. For if it were true, since they have many organs similar to ours, they could make themselves understood to us as to their own kind. It is also a quite remarkable thing that, although there are many animals that show more industry than us in some of their actions, we see, however, that the same animals show none in many others of their actions. Thus, their doing better than us does not prove they have intelligence, because it would hence follow that they would possess more of it than any of us and would do better in everything else; but rather it proves they have none and it is nature that acts in them, according to the disposition of their organs: in the same way, we see that a clock, composed only of wheels and springs, can count the hours and measure the time more precisely than us with all our prudence.

I described after that the rational soul and showed that it can in no way be derived from the potentiality of matter, as can the other things of which I had spoken, but rather it must be expressly created. And I showed how it is not sufficient for it to be lodged in the human body, like a helmsman in his ship, unless perhaps to move its members, but rather it must be more closely joined and united with it, to have in addition feelings and appetites like ours, and thus to constitute a real person. Further, I elaborated here a little on the subject of the soul, because it is of the greatest importance; for, after the error of those who deny God, which I believe I already sufficiently refuted, there is nothing that leads weak minds more from the straight path of virtue than to imagine that the soul of animals is of the same nature as ours, and hence that after this life we have nothing to fear or hope for, any more than flies and ants. But when we know how much animals differ from us, we understand much better the reasons proving that our soul is of a nature entirely independent of the body, and consequently, that it is not bound to die with it. And since we do not see other causes that destroy the soul, we are naturally inclined to judge from this that it is immortal.[25]

---

25. Descartes begins Part VI of the *Discourse on Method* stating, "But it is now three years since I reached the end of the treatise containing all these things and began to review it in order to put it into the hands of a printer, when I learned that people to whom I defer, and whose authority over my actions can hardly be less than that of my own reason over my thoughts, had disapproved of an opinion in physics published a short time before by someone else, about which I do not mean to say that I was in agreement, but rather I had not noticed anything in it before their censure that I could imagine being prejudicial either to religion or to the state, nor consequently anything that would have prevented me from writing it, had reason persuaded me of it; and this made me fear that similarly there might be some among my opinions in which I had been mistaken, notwithstanding the great care I always took not to receive into my beliefs any new opinions for which I did not have very certain demonstrations, and not to write anything that could turn to anyone's disadvantage. This was sufficient to force me to change the resolution I once had to publish my opinions. For, although the reasons for which I had previously made the resolution were very strong, my inclination, which has always made me hate the profession of writing books, made me immediately find enough other reasons to excuse me from it (AT VI, 60)." The treatise he is referring to is again *Le Monde* together with *Man*; the "opinion in physics published a short time before by someone else" is the motion of the earth discussed by Galileo in his *Dialogue Concerning the Two Chief World Systems*, 1632.

C. SUMMARY OF DESCARTES, *DESCRIPTION OF THE HUMAN BODY*[26]

The Description of the Human Body and all its Functions, both those not depending on the Soul as well as those depending on it. And also, the main cause of the formation of its bodily members

Part I. Preface

1. That it is very useful for medicine to know well the functions of our body (p. 223).
2. How it happens that it is customary to attribute these functions to the soul (p. 224).
3. Why they should not be attributed to it.
4. Another reason that proves the same thing (p. 225).
5. That although these functions cease at death, it does not follow that they depend on the soul.
6. That one does not need to have studied much anatomy to understand this treatise (p. 226).
7. Summary of things the treatise will contain.

Part II. The motion of the heart and blood

8. That there is heat in the heart and its nature (p. 228).
9. Description of the parts of the heart.
10. How the heart and the arteries move (p. 231).
11. The motion of the heart auricles and the cause of their structure (p. 233).
12. Description of the vena cava.
13. The arterial vein, the venous artery, and the lungs (p. 235).
14. The use of the lungs (p. 235).
15. The openings in infants' hearts (p. 237).

---

26. These section and article titles are by Clerselier, from his 1664 edition of *L'Homme de René Descartes*; the page references are to the AT edition of the *Description of the Human Body*.

16. The great artery and the circulation of the blood (p. 238).
17. Reasons that demonstrate this circulation (p. 239).
18. Refutation of Harvey regarding the motion of the heart, with proofs of the real opinion (p. 241).

Part III. Nutrition

19. That some parts of the blood issue from the arteries when they swell (p. 245).
20. That the bodies with life are only composed of continually flowing small filaments or rivulets (p. 247).
21. How when young we increase in size (p. 248).
22. How we gain and lose weight (p. 249).
23. How we age and die of old age (p. 250).
24. Of the two causes that determine a part of the liquid to render itself to the part of the body it is fit to nourish.
25. How the first cause acts (p. 251).
26. How the other cause acts.

Digression, in which the Formation of the Animal is treated

Part IV. The bodily parts formed in the seed

27. The nature of the seed (p. 252).
28. How the heart begins to be formed (p. 253).
29. How the heart begins to move (p. 254).
30. How blood is made.
31. Why blood is red (p. 255).
32. Why blood is redder than coals or a hot iron (p. 256).
33. How the great artery and the vena cava begin to be formed.
34. How the right cavity of the heart is formed (p. 257).
35. How the lung and its three vessels begin to be formed (p. 259).
36. The nature of aerial particles.
37. Why a third cavity does not form in the heart (p. 260).

38. How the brain begins to be formed (p. 261).
39. How the sense organs begin to be formed.
40. Why they are double (p. 262).
41. Where their difference comes from.
42. Smell, sight, hearing, and taste.
43. Touch (p. 263).
44. Why most body parts are double (p. 264).
45. Why the nerves issue differently from the first two junctures of the spinal column than from the others (p. 265).
46. Why some nerves issue immediately from the head.
47. Why many issue from the backbone.
48. How the arteries and veins both extend their branches throughout the whole body (p. 266).
49. Why we see fewer arteries than veins (p. 267).
50. How the coronary arteries and veins are formed (p. 268).
51. How the veins and arteries that go to the arms are formed.
52. How the great triangular vessel is formed (p. 269).
53. How the *rets admirabilus* is formed (p. 270).
54. How the *infundibulum* and choroid tissues are formed.
55. Why the veins and the arteries do not distribute themselves in the same way (p. 271).
56. Why a severed limb does not impede circulation.
57. Why the carotid arteries are double.
58. Why the left spermatic vein comes from the emulgent vessel (p. 272).
59. Why the mammary and epigastric arteries and veins join, veins to veins and arteries to arteries.

Part V. The formation of the solid parts

60. That the navel is the last part to be formed from the seed (p. 273).
61. What the matter of the solid parts is (p. 274).
62. How this matter begins to compose the membranes of the arteries.

63. How the filaments, which the solid members are composed of, begin to form (p. 275).
64. That the filaments have their roots along the arteries.
65. What the reason is for believing that the membranes of the veins are formed from the blood they contain (p. 276).
66. That from the knowledge of the parts of the seed we can deduce the shape and structure of all bodily members.
67. How the heart enlarges and perfects itself (p. 277).
68. How the fibers of the heart are formed (p. 278).
69. What the cause of the small valves at the entrances to the vena cava and venous artery is.
70. The causes of the small valves at the outlets to the great artery and the arterial vein (p. 279).
71. What the general cause of the production of the small valves is.
72. In what the heat of the heart consists, and how its motion is produced (p. 280).
73. Where does the shape and consistency of the heart come from (p. 282).
74. How the pericardium and all the other skins, membranes, and surfaces of the body are formed (p. 283).